The PENDULUM
Bridge to Infinite Knowing

Beginning through Advanced Instructions

by Dale W. Olson

Crystalline Publications
Eugene, Oregon

Crystalline Publications
P.O. Box 2088
Eugene, Oregon 97402

First Printing February 1997

Manufactured in The United States of America

ISBN #1-879-246-08-2
Library of Congress Catalog Card # 90-837111

Dedication

May this book assist you in knowing your Intuition, the part of you that is connected to the Infinite source of all Love, Light, Knowledge, and Wisdom.

Acknowledgements

Special recognition and thanks to Doctor Marcel Vogel, who was a great scientist, inventor, healer, and teacher. It was a great privilege to have studied with such a wise, loving, and consciously aware human being. He has been a great inspiration in broadening my parameters of knowledge, and a great catalyst in bringing our expanded abilities out of the dark ages through applied science. Personally, his light in healing my heart is beyond words and value, and his help in igniting the light within will be of great value to many.

I give further thanks to Doctor Rudy Zupancic who has been not only a great friend, but also a great influence in showing me that it is the Intuition that separates the health care professionals from the true healers.

Most of all I Am grateful to Johanna Keller who helped me beyond measure by introducing the pendulum and other tools that enabled me to bridge the connection with the Intuition.

I would like to give my greatest appreciation to Judith Marie Pleskow for all of her great work in bringing this book into form through her endless love, support, and great artistic talents.

I give special thanks and appreciation to the editors Laura Walden, Dennis Sanfilippo and my limitless thanks and love to Kalani Honua Goins, my spiritual twin, who took the time from writing her own book to make this book whole.   Heartfelt Thanks

Note from the Author

I am often asked how I became involved with the development of intuitive skills. Over 20 years ago, I found myself entangled in the trials of life. Feeling confused and not knowing the "how to", and the "where to from here", I felt compelled to consult a very wise, elderly "psychic," Johanna Keller. One day, after having had several enlightening sessions with her, she turned to me and said, "Dale, you don't need to come to me for the answers, for you already have all the answers within you." Of course, I had heard this dozens of times before in numerous teachings that I had found in books and tapes. Nonetheless, the same old questions popped up in my mind, "Yes, but how do you get to that information," or "How do you know when you *know*?" At that moment, Johanna said, "Dale, I'm going to give you two tools to help you find the answers for yourself; the Pendulum and a three-card method for verification." This was the beginning of my work which would involve creating the space in which the intuitive knowing could come to the conscious state. Through these techniques I would learn how to externalize the Intuition beyond my subconscious mind. I was starting at the elementary level, yet for the first time I was able to open the lines of communication and have direct, conscious connection between the self that I was aware of and the Intuition that seemed so intangible. In the years that followed, these techniques and others proved to be a very precise and accurate means which would help me to bring the light to that which had been unknown.

One of the highlights of my intuitive development occurred over 16 years ago in the Cascade Mountains of Oregon. The Bohemia Mining District within the Umpqua National Forest, has been my home away from home and is nature at it's best. It is also rich in gold mining history and lore dating back to the Gold Rush era of the mid 1800's. My journey there laced together many lessons and adventures.

Years ago I headed into these mountains with nothing more than desire, a set of dowsing rods, a pendulum, and a belief that I would find gold. At the time, I knew absolutely nothing about prospecting, mineralogy, geology, mining or anything else of the sort. I set out to see what I could do with my intuitive abilities. To shorten a long story, by the end of that summer I had established two hard-rock mining claims and seven placer mining claims amounting to approximately 180 acres of mining operations. I had located both nugget gold in the river beds and also gold-bearing quartz veins. I had also learned a great deal about prospecting, mineralogy, mining, and geology. My dreams had helped to generate the idea of prospecting, mining and the general area where it should begin. The dowsing rods showed me the "where" and the pendulum assisted me in finding the specific area, depth, the exact place to start digging, and the potential amount of gold-bearing ore. I added *persistence, determination, and trust* to the tools I was using to help me find my way. In doing so, my success proved that we can use our Intuition to find something of which we have had no prior knowledge. I also proved that we are able to fine-tune our capacities to detect the subtle energies of metals such as gold and silver that may be 50' to 150' below the surface of the ground. Now *that* thought is quite mind-expanding! My desire for an adventure had been fulfilled, and most important, I found that I could successfully use my intuitive capacities to find gold.

During my adventure I learned significant lessons about illusion and visions of grandeur. The incredibly hard work of mining helped to put the deluding effects of "gold fever" into proper perspective. I never knew there could be so many forms of iron pyrite (fools gold). As they say, "All that glitters is not gold;" a very valuable lesson to keep in mind when making choices that will have long range impacts on one's life. I did end up with assay reports indicating beyond any question of a doubt that I had found gold and silver-bearing ore of valid proportions. However, these reports indicated a grade of ore not high enough to warrant the exorbitant cost of setting up a mining and milling operation. Thus, such an operation would be financially impractical. At that time, my desire said to go for further exploration, but my Intuition was telling me to stop. In reality this great adventure was one of the most dangerous things I could be doing with my life: working with high explosives, close calls with cave-ins, breathing in quartz dust (which is worse than asbestos), and other dangers were large stop signs in the road. My choice was to end the mining operation.

It took a great deal of strength to put aside my invested interest, desire, and visions of grandeur to listen to that small inner voice of my Intuition saying, "That was a great adventure that you will never forget, and you found what you were looking for. Now it's time to get on with your life's work—and mining for a living is not part of it." I trusted that information, realizing that the Intuition was a good indicator that I was getting away from my life's chosen direction for too long, and that I was subjecting myself to risks that were not for my highest and greatest benefit.

I did not fulfill my visions of grandeur or reap great financial riches; nonetheless, it was a rewarding period in the development of my Intuition and I will always have fond memories of a grand adventure that made the whole experience very rich. This experience had given me practice, confidence and trust in developing my intuitive skills which I could now apply to all aspects of my life.

I came out of the mountains and began to work in other realms using my Intuition as a guide. My advanced work with the Intuition as it pertains to the health care profession has been inspired by training with Doctors Rudy Zupancic, Benoytosh Bhattacharyya, and Marcel Vogel. After working with Rudy Zupancic for years in his healing practice, I learned that effective healing takes highly developed communications with both the Intuition as well as the patient in order to access the source or cause of the symptoms, dis-ease, or dis-order.

From Benoytosh Bhattacharyya, I learned that it is possible to analyze and treat an individual with a dis-order or dis-ease at a distance.

Dr. Marcel Vogel was truly one of the great scientists, inventors and teachers of our times. His work is reflected throughout the content of this book. The keys he taught include proper use of breath, keeping an open heart and mind as well as a positive mental-emotional model for the joy of living, health and well-being.

After having spent years working with and duplicating their results, I have learned how to use the pendulum and dowsing rods for advanced forms of multidimensional analysis of the human body.

Within every human being there is an innate knowledge of everything that is going on. This includes a complete analysis of the vitamin and mineral content, deficiencies of any kind, and the exact location and source of all disease. Whether the questioning is of a physical, mental, emotional, or spiritual nature, it is only a matter of making the information available to the conscious mind. All information about ourselves is available to us when we learn the art of "fine tuning" through the development of our bridge to the Intuition.

Doctors Zupancic, Bhattacharyya, Vogel, myself and many others agree that there are four main facets to the human "being:" physical, mental, emotional, and spiritual. These aspects can be accurately and completely accessed through the Intuition. The magnitude of this work is incredible, and it is definitely worth one's time and determination to become proficient in developing the expanded skills of the mind.... the Intuition. Through the development of the Intuition, you will find a tenfold increase in the quality of your life, resulting in greater fulfillment of your mind's potential and an increase in your personal awareness and self-worth. A developed Intuition can save time and money, and may prevent many of the unnecessary tribulations suffered by those who choose the trial-and-error approach to life. This savings in time and accuracy in problem-solving allows for an increase in your health, wealth, total well-being and the pursuit of your dreams.

Introduction

We are now in a new age of great technological innovation, and also a time of many consciously aware individuals. Our lives are filled with numbers of daily choices and decisions which will have an impact on all of our futures. If we make our choices and decisions only from our well-developed intellect or the five physical senses, then we are limiting our judgement to basically a trial-and-error, or guessing approach to life.

However, by using the Intuition, we may rise above the trial-and-error approach by acknowledging the pool of infinite knowledge. All we need to do is learn the skills to accurately bridge the connection between the mind and the Intuition.

Our Intuition is the liaison, or doorway, to the Infinite Intelligence. It is through this intermediary that we may draw upon the forces of Infinite Intelligence. It alone contains the secret process by which mental impulses are modified and changed into their spiritual or etheric equivalent. It is the medium through which thought may be directed into prayer, and prayer may be transmitted to the source capable of answering prayer.

Unfortunately, in this day and age, marketing is more concerned with making sales than in pointing to the actual quality or integrity of a new product or service. The labels on products cannot possibly disclose all the information that we, as the consumers, may need to know. The lack of information, or even misinformation, on some products could cost a person his health, and possibly, his life. We can no longer depend only on our rational minds to make the correct decisions when there are so many unknowns concerning these products or services. This "buyer beware" market of both goods and services has made it a necessity to develop a functional Intuition that can accurately and effectively communicate to us what is, and what is not, for our highest and greatest good. It is now a necessity to develop our intuitive abilities in a practical and tangible sense in order to avoid poor choices which could cost us time, money, health, and a decline in the quality of life.

It is no longer necessary to feel the stress that comes from not knowing whether the product that we hold in our hands is toxic, allergenic, ineffective, mildly useful, good, or highly beneficial. Learning how to externalize the Intuition, and being in conscious communication with the Intuition, can raise us above the trial-and-error (guessing) approach to life. The first step is to acknowledge the pool of infinite knowledge available to all of us, and then to learn the skills necessary to accurately access this part of ourselves, the Intuition.

Anyone with proper training, who has a fairly good ability to concentrate and who has reasonable control over his emotional and mental stability, can use the pendulum. With the expanded abilities we can become quite accurate within a relatively short period of time. Remember, we are all born with these abilities of knowing and they manifest in different forms, levels, and degrees. It is a natural ability that we can develop like any other skill, taking only *time* and *practice* to acquire. When we develop the bridge to the Intuition, we learn how to use our mind's great potential to its fullest extent.

Many of you reading this book may, or may not, have had experience in using the pendulum as a tool to consciously access your Intuition. Others of you may already use a pendulum. There is always room for more knowledge and understanding in order to obtain effective and accurate results. It may be helpful for you to disregard some of what you thought you knew about the pendulum and be open to developing a new or different approach to this tool of the Intuition.

An individual's ability to do effective pendulum work may initially vary dramatically. Consequently, we will begin by establishing a fundamental pendulum or dowsing form. For the advanced student, please bear with some of the elementary dialogue. You may also benefit from a new approach to ancient techniques and reminders of methods with which you may already be familiar.

This book contains some general principles designed to promote your personal growth as well as specific techniques to enhance your intuitive work. I would like to assure you that your Intuition works perfectly right now. There is nothing that I, or anyone else, can present to you that will "make it work better." However, by learning good pendulum form, by doing this program and the exercises involved, you *will* develop your ability to identify, value, and trust your Intuition. With practice, you *will* be able to make the connection and effectively access your Intuition and grow beyond a 'hit or miss' or 'trial and error' approach to life.

It is my joy to assist you in developing good pendulum form and teach you how to apply the skill of the Intuition to everyday decision-making and problem-solving. My greatest desire is that this book will assist you in creating a limitless bridge to your Intuition and to increase your quality of life ten-fold.

Table of Contents

Chapter 7

Chapter 8

Chapter 1

The Science and Art of the Pendulum

Tools for the Intuition, including the pendulum, go back to 8000 B.C., and were used by the Hebrews, Egyptians, Chinese, Romans, Greeks, Druids, Hindus, Peruvians, and the American Indians. Even Moses was a skilled dowser, and in the Bible, there are several references to Moses being a "water wizard," which means that he was able to find water for the masses by means of a dowsing staff. The Egyptians were also known for using dowsing rods and pendulums, not only for finding water and gold, but also for divination. The Chinese would call for a *Radiesthesist*, a person adept at using a pendulum or other tools, for sensing the unseen energies around the potential building sites in order to detect, what they called, "The Claw of the Dragon." These correspond to what we now call the harmful rays of a positive-charge vortex or positive-charge ley lines.

Dowsing is the art of using a tool (such as a pendulum or dowsing rod) to access the Intuition and gather information not directly available to the rational thinking part of our conscious mind. It is the coupling of skills used by the intellectual mind to access the Intuition. Dowsing can be accomplished while physically present on site or from a distance about a particular site. This same process can be done with people.

Radiesthesia is defined as the detecting and measuring of an entire spectrum of radiation that may eminate from mineral, plant, animal, or human. 'Divining' includes the art of dowsing and radiesthesia. It speaks to the possibility of knowing beyond the limitations of one's five physical senses, including the sensing of future results or events, with or without the use of a device, cards, or symbols. The goal of dowsing, historically and presently, is to access information not available to our conscious minds from our Intuition through the use of specific tools.

Dowsing is a serious matter, a spiritual matter, and is not to be taken lightly. Obviously, when you are first beginning to dowse, you may not know if your interest will wane, or whether you will continue to dowse as a hobby, or perhaps become a service to others. Whether your desire is to dowse for yourself or to extend your dowsing abilities to include helping others, it is imperative to preface your dowsing work with an affirmation such as, **"Infinite, allow only that which is for the highest and greatest good and well-being for all concerned to prevail."**

As you evolve and become more experienced in dowsing, you may desire to increase your effectiveness and accuracy. You may strive to become more clear and whole. In this way, you may become a channel for the greatest good and benefit. This can only be accomplished by committing to advance in this skill, by learning self-mastery techniques, and by gaining dowsing experience through practice (and more practice). For you to become a successful pendulist or dowser, you will need to learn to develop accurate, consistent, precise communication with your Intuition. You will need to learn about the basic dowsing tool—the pendulum—and how to invite your Intuition and the pendulum to interact skillfully.

The Brain—The Intuition

Dowsing is a way of relating to the earth and the cosmos. It is a way of using the full potential of the brain. We in western society have been conditioned to rely on the rational or left part of the brain almost to the exclusion of the right, or creative/intuitive side of the brain. What this means for most of us is that our lives are filled with goal-oriented, action-oriented, linear, logical, verbal thinking at the expense of our imagination, creativity, and receptivity. Logical/rational thought has become so dominant in our society that it is hard to believe that in some cultures people are strongly encouraged to look to the Intuition for the answers to the unknowns that are beyond the five physical senses. The right side of the brain, home of the Intuition, has been tremendously undervalued and in some cases totally ignored. From earliest childhood, most of us were praised and rewarded for performing mental feats involving logic, memory, and other measurable cognitive skills. Our traditionally biased educational system is based on the belief that quantitatively measurable skills are superior to the skill of using the Intuition or imagination which can only be experienced qualitatively. The difficulty is that along with this rational system comes limiting belief systems such as: trial-and-error, "seeing is believing", cause and effect, and logical, step-by-step

3

reasoning. Unfortunately for some, the rational mind has been developed so profoundly that there is no room for any other ideas resulting in limited or no connection with the Intuition. The old approach, "If you can't measure it, see it, hear it, or touch it, it can't possibly exist," is the first belief system to discard if you want to have intuitive success.

The Intuition may sometimes seem elusive to you. This is because the Intuition occurs in a part of the brain that has no language. To successfully access the Intuition, you must use all aspects of the brain. You must realize that both the left and right hemispheres of your brain are always working and that you can think rationally *and* use your Intuition at the same time. Again, this is not about one side of the brain being better than the other, it is about *co-processing*. You can learn to allow your left brain to put your intuitive insights into words and/or nerve-muscle actions with the pendulum. Dowsing is the perfect marriage of communication between the two sides of your brain. You have the left side, which loves rational, linear thinking, that wants to know what, when, why, and how-a sort of sophisticated computer. The right side, or intuitive part of the brain does not know how to frame questions. It does not have language skills, only *feeling* skills. Language skills are the forte of the left brain. In using the Intuition, it is necessary for the left brain to formulate the words of the questioning in a precise and constant form.

> *In communicating with the Intuition, your accuracy and success is based on one simple guide: your answers will be only as good as your questions.*

In other words, precisely communicated questions presented to your Intuition can provide you with the information to which your rational mind may not have access, and your rational mind can then put that information from the Intuition into words or actions. It is not as difficult as it sounds, it only takes learning good form and practice.

Establishing communication lines between your rational left brain and intuitive right brain begins with the desire to know. Then, allow your rational mind to frame a good question that can be answered by *Yes, No, Maybe*. Then work up to accuracy with degrees of *Yes* and *No* with percentages (___%).

The Pendulum

The pendulum is one of the oldest, most popular, potentially most rewarding, and historically most misunderstood of all tools used by the Intuition. More than any other instrument, it is the one most commonly associated with mystical phenomena, and the occult. There are books that talk about the pendulum as a mysterious device that will lead you to untold fame and fortune, personal fulfillment, and romance. Because of such claims and distortions, you need to remind yourselves that a pendulum is nothing more than an extension of your *own* personal Intuition. A pendulum, whether it is crystal, wooden, metallic, or plastic, is nothing more than a balanced weight on the end of a string or chain. It *does not* have a mind of its own nor is it a part of anyone elses influence unless the dowser uses poor pendulum form, which will be discussed later. The pendulum is nothing more than a device that gives your Intuition a language with which to communicate. It does this through micro-movements of the fingers or hand which are an extension of you, the pendulist. Any response shown by a pendulum comes from you, through you, using your intuitive ability and desire to be receptive. **You** are the one in charge of this skill.

Often we hear people talking about their pendulum giving them the answers as though the pendulum is "picking up" information, or has some degree of mysterious independent intelligence. The pendulum does nothing in and of itself. We need to remind ourselves from time to time that it is our mind, the Intuition and the Infinite source (however you may perceive that to be), which is supplying the answers. We are all interconnected, as though on a gigantic "party line," which explains our ability to get in touch with our Source.

Pendulum Types

A pendulum is a small weight suspended from a chain or string, preferably about 3 to 6 inches in length. The types of pendulums vary immensely, and the various styles have different qualities due to their shape, weight, mass, and size. Some have a fast action because of their light weight and small size. Others have slow movement because of their heavy weight , and do well in windy conditions. A pendulum can be made of almost any substance. Many objects work well, including lead crystal, quartz crystal, wood, plastic, and wooden plumb bobs. Frequently, pendulums are designed with the lower half of the pendulum serving as a kind of pointer. This is helpful when using pendulum charts, because they show degrees of difference which a pointed pendulum can indicate.

The most important factor is that in order to work well, the pendulum needs to have a weight at the end that is centered and balanced so that it can swing freely in all directions free from any built-in directional influence, a "catch," a natural pull one direction or another due to the way it is constructed. Find a pendulum that feels comfortable for you. Remember, its purpose is to assist you in externalizing your Intuition; it is *not* the source of your answers.

When searching for a particular substance such as water, gold, silver, oil, etc., a special type of pendulum with  a screw top and a hollowed-out inside can be used. This type of pendulum serves as a receptacle for a *sample* or *witness* of the substance or object of your search. Additional information on how sample or witness pendulums work is discussed later on in this chapter.

Ways of the Pendulum

There are three basic ways in which to use the pendulum:

1. The pendulum is held directly over an object or body and the questions asked concern the object or body.

2. The pendulum is held over an object (like food) or over a remedy and questions asked regarding the object's benefit to yourself or another.

3. A screw top *sample* pendulum is used to dowse for a like substance. The substance is placed inside the pendulum as a sample or *witness* .

The "Witness Method" makes it possible to work on testing substances or measuring variables for yourself or someone else by the use of samples, maps, photos, diagrams and/or *Pendulum Charts*. (See Pendulum Applications and Distance Dowsing for further details).

The Witness or Sample pendulum is constructed with a hollow section so that the "witness" or sample can be placed inside. Witness items can be samples of water, herbs, flower essences, vitamins, minerals, oil, gold, or a fragment of anything approximating the object of one's inquiry. If one is looking for gold, for example,a gold object or nugget inserted into the pendulum cavity will aid in the dowsing quest.

A *"sample"* is an object or substance related to the object of the search. It is an item associated with the place, person, object or *thing* sought: such as part of the actual treasure or a sample ore specimen previously found at the probable mining site. In the case of a person, the *sample* can be a lock of his/her hair, a bit of fingernail, or an article of jewelry or clothing. When a pet has wandered away, the animal's hair, a collar, or the pet's toy will suffice.

The *witness* or *sample* functions in accordance with the ancient laws of *sympathetic attraction* (like attracts like). Remote locating through *sympathetic attraction* relates closely to the phenomenon of *psychometry*, a method used for gathering information about and from the object in question. *Psychometry* relies on the memory thought form held within the object itself. Most people who do psychometry believe that objects still maintain mental, physical, and environmental memory thought forms that can be accessed by our intuitive mind and then relayed to the conscious mind. The psychometrist attempts to determine the object's appropriate frequency or resonance through inward, mental visualization. This activity is similar to viewing a TV or movie within one's mind with your eyes closed. Once the appropriate frequency or resonance is attuned to, one is often able to see the whole picture of the person, place or event connected with the particular object. Amazing case studies have validated *psychometry* as having scientific value. The relatively new scientific study of psychic archeology is developing with dowsers, psychometrists, and mediums contributing to successful archaeological explorations.

Choosing a Pendulum

Choosing a pendulum may be your first opportunity to trust in that aspect of the Intuition that truly wants that which is most beneficial for you. Allow your inner feeling to make the proper choice. This inner feeling may come in various subtle forms; such as feeling drawn to a

9

particular material, color, texture or weight because it *feels* good, or one may catch your eye through *first impressions*. One may just feel good to hold in your hand, or one may give you a feeling of ease or feel comfortable. We all have the ability to feel these subtle feelings, it is just a matter of being a little out of practice in acknowledging them. The only thing that is really important is that you believe that the pendulum you choose will work for your "highest and greatest benefit."

When you choose a pendulum, you want it to be appropriate for yourself and for the particular dowsing work that you may do. Consequently, you may choose a pendulum with the added features of a quartz crystal, a witness cup, pointer, and/or precision balance. Keep in mind that the pendulum you choose most likely will not be your one and only. Some people find that different pendulums for different applications seem most appropriate. Many pendulist seem to have a variety of pendulums with favorites that are used for various jobs or subject matters. The best guide of all in choosing a pendulum is what *feels* good to you.

Experiment with the string or chain to find the most comfortable length that works for you. Typically, the shorter the string, the faster the action. A heavier weight, however, requires a longer string. Large, heavy pendulums produce less erratic movement while walking. However, you must walk considerably more slowly when using a large pendulum. This gives the instrument time to overcome inertia, and to change directions; otherwise you may find yourself walking over, or past the energy field emanating from the object of the search.

Chapter 2
Pendulum Language

The pendulum is a direct bridge for communication between the conscious and the Intuition. It serves to externalize the Intuition by giving it a language which we can understand. In order for this to take place, we must establish the simple pendulum language between the various parts of the brain. This takes some time and practice. You will need to develop the language which will indicate *Yes* or *No* as well as a way to measure degrees or percentages.

The direction or action of the pendulum requires coordination and cooperation between the left and right part of the brain and then in relaying that message to the part of the brain that can deliver the appropriate response to your arm, hand, finger tips and the pendulum.

Pendulums are incredibly versatile in the way they assist in communicating with your Intuition. Consequently, they can respond in numerous ways. This can cause some unnecessary misunderstanding and confusion. This is because many people will use the pendulum without consciously developing a precise and consistent form of communication, a language between the conscious mind, the subconscious, the Intuition and the pendulum. Remember that any response shown by the pendulum comes from you and is a reflection of the degree of proficiency in developing the bridge with your Intuition. **You** are the one in charge of this learning experience. Please be patient with yourself and this process for as with developing any skill, it takes time and practice.

Developing a pendulum language is a matter of training your conscious mind to work correctly and accurately with the Intuition. As part of the pendulum language you want the body to have automatic responses to the questions you are asking. That will cause the pendulum to move in a variety of predetermined patterns which will begin to show you the shades of meaning beyond the simple *"Yes"* or *"No"* answers. Most often, answers fall into a category of greater-or-lesser degrees of *"Yes" or "No"* rather than strict *"Yes"* or *"No"* answers. Therefore, the way in which you develop the language with your pendulum is very important.

Pendulum Attunement & Language Development

"Identifying" means setting up the language between your conscious mind and the Intuition, the energetics of the body, and the subtle muscle movement of the hand and fingers that will cause the pendulum to move. The language is comprised of six directions: forward and  backward, side-to-side, clockwise and counter- clockwise,

ovals, or a motion somewhere in-between forward-and-backward or side-to-side movement.

Begin to use the pendulum by first holding the string or chain in the hand you use to write with (this is your dominant hand.) Hold the string of the pendulum between your thumb and forefinger with your wrist slightly arched so that the pendulum can have a direct drop. Seek that which is comfortable for you. For some people, using the opposite of the dominant hand may be more appropriate. Experiment with both hands until you find which hand is more comfortable and which works more effectively for you. The pendulum can now move easily back-and-forth, side-to-side or in a circular motion.

Your first step is to align yourself with the pendulum. This means that you must find the length of the string or chain and the "hold position" that will result in the pendulum having the most natural swing for you. Start by holding the string close to the weight at the end of the pendulum. Begin to swing your pendulum gently back-and-forth as you *slowly* let out the string with your thumb and index finger. Once the pendulum starts moving, just let it continue without pushing it. Just watch it. Can you *feel* it working with the natural movement of your hand, or do you find yourself restarting the swing continuously? After you have let the string out an inch or two, allow the pendulum to circle in either a clockwise or counterclockwise direction. Adjust the length of the string or chain several times until you find the length where the pendulum needs no effort from you to keep going once started. Sometimes the pendulum will seemingly go into a particular motion without your assistance and that is okay because for now we are just trying different ways of holding the pendulum to find what *feels* best for you.

Pendulum Language Techniques

Now that you have aligned your pendulum with your choice of hand, string length, and its motion, it is time to establish the language between your conscious mind, the Intuition, and the pendulum.

All pendulum work begins with an oscillating position referred to by dowsers as the neutral, or "search" mode. The most common is a back-and-forth swing of the pendulum. For some, it may be a side-to-side motion, or a clockwise or counterclockwise motion. The important consideration is that you establish a neutral position that works best for you.

Developing Your Pendulum Language

First Exercise: Begin your practice by first holding your pendulum in whatever way you've found comfortable. Swing it gently back and forth so that it feels like it's moving by itself. Do all the following movements by first asking the Intuition and all parts involved to move the pendulum, imaging it moving in those directions rather than pushing it or making it do so. Now ask it to change the movement to go in a clockwise direction. Then ask it to return to a back and forth motion. Now ask for a counterclockwise movement, and then back to a neutral or back-and-forth direction. Next, try a side-to-side movement, and finally, a diagonal direction.

The next step is to assign *meaning* to these various movements such as "Yes" and "No" or "Positive" and "Negative."

Second Exercise: This exercise can help you establish greater depth with your pendulum movements and give meaning to them. This is a *polarity awareness* exercise.

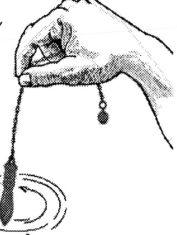

• Start by finding a quiet place, free from any distraction. Sit in a chair with your body in good posture, your knees apart and feet on the floor.

•Hold your pendulum between your knees and start it swinging gently away from and then directly toward you (back-and-forth).

• In the beginning, if your pendulum doesn't seem to go back and forth of its own accord, make it do so.

The *Yes* or Positive Response:

• Now hold the pendulum directly over your right knee. The pendulum for most people will start to circle in a clockwise direction. This is a *"Yes"* response. Clockwise, for most is *Yes*. The clockwise rotation of the *"Yes"* response may also be referred to as positive, (+), male, solar, active, or yang.

The *No* or Negative Response:

• Now hold the pendulum directly over the left knee. The pendulum will start to circle in a counterclockwise direction. This is a *"No"* response. Counterclockwise direction for most is *No*. The counterclockwise rotation of the "no" response may also be referred to as negative, (-), female, lunar, passive, or yin.

15

The pendulum responds in these ways because we are a composite of all the above aspects, not necessarily one or the other. If you have different motions or responses to the exercises, ask and *feel* whether these differences are the result of a lack in your current language or a matter of having a different or unique form to your language. There is no right or wrong way to establish direction of swing, because to the Intuition, it does not matter. It is your language that you are establishing and the only real importance is that it *feels* good to you and it will work to do all that you want. If your are already using a different language than the one outlined above, stay with it. Continue to use the one you have already established. It doesn't make any difference what language or code you use for your responses, just as long as you are precise, consistent, and it does all that you want with your communications. However, once you establish a direction or pattern it is very difficult to change. You may want to start by stating "These are the directions which I want to be associated with these words and meanings." For the beginner, the following will help in establishing the most commonly used pendulum language.

• If your pendulum doesn't seem to gyrate naturally in a clockwise direction over the right knee and a counterclockwise rotation over the left knee, then make it move yourself. All we are doing is setting up a consistent language associated with pendulum directions between your conscious and Intuition. For a minute or so, hold the pendulum over your right knee, watch it rotate in a clockwise direction, and say to your self, "This means *Yes*."

• Now hold your pendulum over your left knee. This time, the pendulum will start to rotate in a counter-clockwise direction. Again, if your pendulum doesn't seem to want to gyrate in a counterclockwise direction, make it do so. Continue holding the pendulum over your left knee, watching it rotate in a counterclockwise direction and say, "This means *No.*"

Pay no attention to any other movement at this time; work only on a *"Yes"* or *"No"* response. The Intuition communicates principally by impressions, imagery, symbols, and feelings when sending or receiving data. Therefore, it is most helpful to instruct your mind as to your *intent.* The key here is to remember you must send the *"Yes"* emphatically with every available impression and feeling possible. For example, use body language with a nod of your head with *"Yes"*, and side to side for *"No."* **If you had some difficulty with the previous exercise in establishing your *Yes/No* directions, do the following exercise.**

Exercise Three: Write on two pieces of paper the words "Yes" and "No."

• Hold your pendulum comfortably and let your pendulum swing in a neutral direction over the "Yes" paper.

• Now focus on "Yes". Affirm anything that goes with "Yes" and build the image.

• Now ask your Intuition and all parts associated with creating your pendulum language to indicate through the pendulum what movement, direction or gyration (clockwise, counterclockwise, back and forth or side-to-side) means "Yes". What is the response in relationship

17

to your image? Try this two or three times. When you are certain as to what the appropriate "Yes" response looks and feels like for you then continue doing the same to find the "No" response.

Fourth Exercise: The next step in developing your pendulum language is to apply your established directions and to expand these parameters in a linear perspective. This may sound more difficult than it really is. You can determine all six pendulum language directions with the following exercise:

• Draw a six-inch circle on a piece of paper with a crisscross in the center, dividing the circle into four sections. (See <u>Pendulum Charts,</u> and use the *Pendulum Language Chart.*)

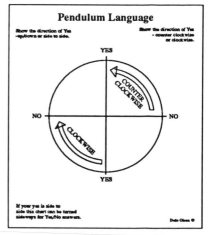

• Give the pendulum a 3-6 inch length on the string and hold it directly over the intersection on your circle or the *Pendulum Language Chart.* Knowing Your Intuitive Mind: Pendulum Charts by Dale Olson, Crystalline Publications, Eugene, OR.

• Look at the chart, remove your attention from the pendulum; focus the intention of your mind to establish the pendulum language.

• Being precise, specific, positive, and declarative with the communication to your subconscious mind is absolutely imperative for success and accurate results. It helps to speak the intentions out loud. For example,

"Intuitive Mind, please indicate the direction of 'Yes' for me." Again, for most people this would be indicated by either a backward and forward swing, or a right-handed or clockwise gyration. For most people a side-to-side swing, or a counterclockwise direction indicates a "No" answer.

• A swing that is in-between can indicate more-or-less, "maybe," or "rephrase the question." Direct your mind and pendulum into action by verbally making your statement: "Intuition, or Infinite Intelligence, indicate to me which direction is for "Maybe", "More-or-Less", "Rephrase the question", and so on. Most often this is indicated by a swing between the back-and-forth and the side-to-side direction (a 45-degree angle to the crisscross on your circle).

Within a short period of time you will reach a stage where you can look at the pendulum and ask the Intuition to indicate Yes, No, Maybe, or More-or-Less and the pendulum will respond immediately.

If at any point there is little or no movement, relax, breathe in and out several times and try again. For some people, the pendulum responds immediately. For others, much patience is needed for the communication to become established. If you get answers slowly, it can be helpful to cup your hands around running water, or place a quartz crystal in your hand for few minutes and try again. This will help you to increase your energetic level and facilitate more success with your pendulum work.

If you find that your pendulum does not move at all, or it moves inconsistently, then consider:

• Are you tired?

- Forcing the situation?

- Focusing too heavily on the pendulum itself?

- Mind wandering and not focusing on the objective?

- Feeling any mental or emotional imbalance?

- Is there a more appropriate time to do this?

- Is there a more appropriate place to be working on this?

- Is there a more appropriate way to state the question?

If any of these points ring true, then release yourself and approach it at another time.

If there is a problem with lack of movement, perhaps it is a matter of too much focus on the pendulum. If there is too much attention of the mental and/or emotional mind involved in trying to make this process work than you may have difficulty in getting the pendulum to work consistently. Most often, success requires a decrease in the focus of the mental and emotional mind. In other words, if you find yourself staring at the pendulum, then you are giving too much focus to the pendulum and would be focused too much from your mental mind. The unfocused state that we refer to can be achieved more easily by holding your elbow tucked against your waist to the side of your body, wrist arched with your pendulum hanging freely so that the pendulum is seen more out of your peripheral vision than by direct sight.

Erratic patterns are occasionally difficult to figure out; however, the confusion is not with the instrument, but within your own mind. The clarity with which you stated your questions or in the degree to which you are able to hold your attention to your objective is paramount. *Your answers will be only as clear as your questions.* This is why we recommend that you keep your pendulum language simple at the beginning and remain focused exclusively on one object.

If you have experienced difficulty with the use of the pendulum, don't give up. Anyone can dowse if they are open to it and determined to be successful with it. Do these first four exercises (establishing movement between your knees with the pendulum, and the Pendulum Language Chart exercise) for seven minutes every day for a week. You will excel rapidly if you practice, and the movement will become second nature. All that is required is a relaxed state of mind and practice along with the willingness to act as though the pendulum will respond independently. If nothing happens, go back to moving it consciously and reminding yourself which motion denotes *"Yes"* and which one means *"No."* If tension or frustration begins to take over, stop for a while and resume the practice later.

If you still have problems, look at your belief systems about the work, learn how to balance and unfocus the mental rational mind, choose a different location or time to do your pendulum exercises, and make sure your area is free of distractions. (See mental and emotional interference.)

Number Priority

In addition to the *Yes, No, Maybe, or More-or-Less* inquiry, the pendulum language may be expanded by means of numbers, letters of the alphabet, and positive

(+) or negative (-) responses. Other refinements will develop as your communication skills improve.

The following form of pendulum language establishes a way to use numbers as a means to measure or gauge any variables for the purpose of comparison between two subjects. This can apply to anything from consumer products to services, events, or any other form of choice-making.

Begin by carefully establishing in your mind the *Yes, No and Maybe* replies. Then, when you're ready, the following method will assist you in finding the correct number answer(s).

• Decide in advance the number scale you wish to work with. For example: you can count it on a 1-10 scale, or multiples of ten (10-100, or 100-1000). Keep your mind clearly focused on the particular number scale you are counting *and* the object of your measurement.

• First construct a question in your mind concerning something simple that you would like to measure. For example: "Intuitive mind, or Infinite Intelligence, to what degree is the food in front of me for my highest and greatest benefit?"

• Start your pendulum oscillating in the *Maybe* position between the forward-and-backward and the side-to-side directions. Present your question to the Intuition. For example, using multiples of 10, start your count 10, 20, 30, 40, 50, 60, and at 60 the pendulum begins to deviate from the *Maybe* position moving towards the *Yes* position. Now start counting backwards until the pendulum resumes the *Maybe* direction... 60, 50, keep going to 40 until the pendulum goes back to the *Maybe* mode. Now go back to 50, and note that the pendulum resumes the *Yes* position. In this case, 50 is the correct measurement or answer to the question. This will be discussed in greater detail in the sections on how to set up parameters of questions and how to work with the using percentages and the *Percentage Chart.*

Alphabet Mode

Developing your pendulum language to include the alphabet will assist you in determining something unknown by finding a letter, or spelling out a name, word, phrase, etc.. This is not to be confused with the similar system associated with the Ouija board. The difference is that the source of the answers of a Ouji board could come from all sorts of influences outside of yourself that may or may not be of the light or that which is for your highest and greatest benefit. This application is asking that the source *only* be from your Intuition. This will be discussed in more detail later on in this book.

• Start the swing of your pendulum in the *Maybe* position (for most, between the forward-and-backward and side-to-side positions).

• Mentally create the question: "The name of my guide or teacher begins with the letter A...? B...? C...? etc...".

• Watch for any change in the pendulum's motion. For example, start with A...? B...? C...? D...? E...? F...? G...? and stay with the process until the pendulum begins to deviate from the *Maybe* mode to the forward-and-backward position... keep going to H...? and again, the pendulum begins to deviate to the *Maybe* position. Now go back to the G, and see that the pendulum resumes the *Yes* position. In this case, G is the correct first letter of the name or the answer to the question. Continue the process until you feel that you have all the letters needed to answer you question or when your pendulum begins to go into another type of movement. An example of this would be a clockwise gyration indicating a *Yes* and complete, or counterclockwise indicating *No* and start over. The previous examples are the types of refinements that you can add to your pendulum language as you develop.

With patience, you can develop letters into names, words, phrases, addresses and even sentences very quickly. In this way you can form word meanings from the Intuition through the letter-symbol language. For additional information see the section on *Alphabet-Numerical Pendulum Chart*.

Pendulum Language for Checking Objects

As you become more proficient with the pendulum and the language between your conscious, subconscious mind and the Intuition, you will find a system that works for you. As you develop an alert dowsing sensitivity, your pendulum will respond readily to your questioning. Whenever you hold the pendulum over any object, animate or inanimate, you will pick up the radiation or vibration from it and the pendulum will usually begin to oscillate.

• Always begin with the *search* mode of a forward-and-backward swing. This commonly signifies the neutral

swing, which merely puts you in contact with the object.
• After you ask a question in relationship to an object, the pendulum will start rotating. For most people, if it rotates to the right or clockwise, it is saying "*Yes*"; this is the positive swing, indicating a positive or harmonious condition. If it rotates to the left, counterclockwise, it is usually saying "*No*"; this is a negative swing, indicating negative or inharmonious condition. The degree to which the pendulum rotates will indicate the extent of your answer. If you ask a question which does not have a *Yes* or *No* answer, or if the question is confusing, or if it doesn't have an answer at all, then the pendulum will oscillate side-to-side indicating a "*No*" answer. It is also possible that there is a third answer being "Maybe", which is in between the*Yes* and *No* position at a 45 degree angle. The *Maybe* position can also mean rephrase the question. You may have made a mistake in how you asked the question. Try rephrasing your question.

First Exercise: Checking for Direction and Polarity

• Hold your pendulum over the top of your left hand. If the pendulum language is being used consistently, the top of your left hand will cause the pendulum to gyrate in a clockwise motion indicating a positive energy.

• Now turn your left hand over, palm up and check; this most likely will cause the pendulum to gyrate in a counterclockwise motion, indicating a negative or receptive energy. You will experience the opposite findings if you hold the pendulum in your left hand and use your right hand for the test.

Second Exercise: Check for Accuracy

• Create five separate papers with mathematical

calculations, some correct and some with errors.

• Mix them up, place them face down on a table, and find the correct ones through positive (+) or clockwise gyration of your pendulum and the incorrect ones by negative (-) or counter-clockwise direction.

This can be a helpful test. However, we find that our abilities work best when we have a good reason for working with the object being tested. If you are trying to trick the Intuition or question its validity, you will most likely get inaccurate answers. This would be an indication of lack in trust and your answers would reflect this.

The following tests are for developing accurate communication lines, and need to be viewed as exercises for practice and developmental purposes.

Third Exercise: Check for Self-tuning or Sensitivity

• This is a good test to do at various times under various conditions. Stand erect, facing due West, relax as much as possible, place your left hand directly over your solar plexus (area from bottom of rib cage to a few inches above navel), palm inward with the fingers closed.

• Suspend the pendulum from the right hand, using the full length of the string so that the pendulum is opposite the center of the left hand and about 8 inches straight out from the left hand.

• Due to the polarity in the area of the solar plexus, for most people, the pendulum will start to gyrate in a clockwise direction or whatever direction your pendulum language indicates for *Yes*. Count the number of gyrations carefully. When the pendulum's movement begins to show a noticeable change in its direction or behavior, make a note of the number of gyrations prior to the pendulum's change.

The degree of sensitivity and strength is indicated by the number of gyrations, and although they vary considerably from individual to individual, they can be grouped roughly as follows: 15-30 weak, 30-50 medium, and 50-100 good. These figures represent the number of complete gyrations and not per minute. If the gyrations are weak and less than fifteen, your chances of getting totally reliable results are remote. Try another time or place.

This is an interesting test. It indicats that the human body is extremely sensitive to outside influences and can be measured accordingly. With practice and patience, you will notice an increase in your dowsing abilities and your sensitivity level.

Fourth Exercise: Checking for Direction

When you are outdoors, your pendulum can be used to indicate where North is.

• Hold your left arm up, and if you have a set of keys, hold them in your left hand between your first and third finger, dangling downwards (which will act as an antenna), and point with your left index finger.

• Hold your pendulum in your right hand, and slowly turn around in a circle. Start the pendulum swing in the *Maybe* mode position. Pay close attention to the pendulum swing as you turn your body. The pendulum will start to move to the *Yes* position as you approach North. If you go past the North position, the pendulum will again start to move back to the *Maybe* position.

The pendulum indicates direction because you are working with the electromagnetic energy of the earth, which runs North and South. Do check this technique for accuracy with a compass. If you don't get completely accurate results, keep practicing until the inner calibration with your Intuition match the external compass.

Fifth Exercise: Finding Lost or Misplaced Objects

Have a friend hide your keys somewhere in your house. Practice using a stream of precise, consistent questions and your pendulum to determine *Yes/No* responses to find out where the keys have been hidden. Remember, the questions must be simple and precise so that a simple *Yes* or *No* response will work. For example; Are the keys in my bedroom?, Yes. Continue with a smaller area; Are my keys in/on/under my dresser? This is not a *Yes/No* question, it is three questions. Keep it simple. Finding of misplaced objects can be a little tricky for beginners and even advanced students. Nonetheless, this exercise makes for good practice.

The more kinds of exercises you do with your pendulum the greater depth you will have in your pendulum language. The more you practice, the greater the precision you will have in the way you phrase questions and inevitably you will be able to determine what areas you may have a natural affinity for and what areas need improvement.

Once you have established the communication and pendulum language with your Intuition, you can expand your development by continuing to work with the preceeding exercises or coming up with your own exercises so that you can check your results. With practice, you will acquire a *feel* for the pendulum, and we suggest that you not go on to more advanced questions until you consistently get accurate results to questions for which you already know the answers. In this way you will establish a consistent language with your Intuition. It takes time and patience to develop these abilities because it takes time for the Intuition to tune into the information requested and for the different parts of your being to become familiar with the language of the pendulum and the various aspects of your consciousness. It also takes time to get to a point of relaxation which, of course, helps all intuitive work.

There is a certain amount of calm or relaxation that comes as you develop the *feel* that goes with your *Yes/No* or directions response. As you develop, you will find yourself getting answers much faster when you know by the *feel* what the answer will be by the kind of movement that the pendulum *begins* to make. There is a lot you can learn by watching the degree of the pendulum's response. The speed at which it responds as well as the magnitude of the response can be a gauge in determining your answers. Sometimes for example, the *Yes/No* response can have such an emphatic or intense swing to it that it makes the response unquestionable, while at other times the response can be a half-hearted wobble.

You may find it helpful to keep a logbook to record the results of your exercises, experiments, or experiences. You may record the time of day, the direction you were facing, what is going on in your environment, the specific questions you asked your Intuition and the answers you received. In this way, you may refer back to the questions in order to enhance your communication and/or to discover errors. The record can also help you to discover the areas in which you are most accurate or proficient. When first learning how to work with a pendulum, you may find yourself giving more attention to the movements than is needed. In time you will find yourself paying less attention to the movements of the pendulum and seeing it more from an unfocused or peripheral perspective. This unfocused state or peripheral perspective is essential in learning and expanding one's intuitive abilities. As you learn to identify and make this shift in state of conscious awareness you will find yourself becoming more aligned or attuned to the very subtle and abstract levels of intuitive work.

In Summary I would like to emphasize that whatever your level of development may be, it is imperative that your pendulum language be precise and consistent and used with clear intention while asking your questions. Remember, your answers will be only as good as your questions. With time and practice, the pendulum will become a true extension of you. You are the context. You are part of the way the question is phrased. Everything you say, think, do, or expect is part of the context. Those are the components that you need to be aware of and monitor as you learn and develop this skill.

In the next chapter we will be working with sucessful form and the importance of releasing or neutralizing any preconceived thoughts or assumptions that may come in to your conscious or subconscious mind while doing your pendulum work which could impact your results.

Chapter 3

Successful Form

How Dowsing Works

There is no magic about dowsing though what can come from it can feel like magic. Most, if not all, of us have the ability to create communication lines with the Intuition. The dowser, with the aid of a physical instrument and a previously determined language, poses a question to the Intuition for the purposes of gathering information regarding a person, plant, animal, substance, time or place. The answer comes from the Intuition, beyond the limitations of one's logical and reasoning processes, though one's intellect does initiate the activity and eventually summarizes the findings.

From one point of view, dowsing involves neuromuscular action. Automatism, as applied to dowsing, implies that thought energy registering in the brain travels through the nervous system. It also suggests that we have the ability to receive rays of light or waves of sound that surround all of us, and all objects. These impulses are then sent down the ulnar nerve causing muscular reflexes in one's fingertips to move the pendulum without conscious physical control. This concept indicates, as previously stated, that the pendulum is only a tool; a symbolic physical device moved by the forces of focused, mental and neuromuscular energy. Scientific tests have shown that there is an increased electrical tension on the skin of a dowser when he/she approaches the object being inquired about. The Intuition is able to search for the answer and send its message to the conscious mind by creating the electrical tension that causes the muscular movement which makes the pendulum respond.

Another theory about the way in which dowsing works is that of *sympathetic resonance*. This theory suggests that traces of a substance, gold for example, within the dowser's body will resonate with the gold in the ground. This specific *resonance* can be felt down to the cellular level. Consequently, a sympathetic vibration and energy flow between the two sources of gold and the subconscious mind create a neuromuscular response that activates the pendulum. This theory implies that as long as the dowser's inquiring mind makes the connecting link between like substances, the distance is unimportant. The range of this technique appears limitless.

The human body is electrical and magnetic in nature, and consequently, it is sensitive and able to register the multitude of electromagnetic forms of energy. When you think about being able to attune yourself or to come into sympathetic resonance with something, know that this extraordinary capacity is already a part of your being.

Communication Skills—Forming Questions

All movement is dependent on communication. We are in continual communication with ourselves and all of life. One can communicate with any life-form, object, or substance providing that clear intention and/or visualized thoughts are formed and held in one's mind-focus. "One mind focus" takes some practice for most of us to acquire because so often we are thinking of many things at one time or flip-flopping back and forth with our thoughts.

The clarity of the query is foremost: incomplete, ambiguous, or hazy questions will bring about confused or wrong answers. *Successful development of this skill lies in finding not the right answers but the right questions.* The questioning is a flow in which each answer leads you to a new question. It is learning how to phrase your questions so that *Yes, No* and percentage (%) questions can make sense. It is easy to slip up with a double question such as, "Do I go left or right?", or a double negative like, "Was the last answer wrong?" in which *No* could be either *No* or *No*-means negative and it was meaning false, *not* wrong.

As adults, many of us want to run with a new skill before we have learned how to walk. It takes much practice to learn good form which leads to knowing how to let the questions flow in a stream. In more advanced work this will feel like juggling a six-level chess game with ease. In the beginning your inquiring mind may need to restate the question frequently to find the correct form which will create flow to your questions. Always ask one inquiry or question at a time. Multiple questions by the unskilled pendulist frequently produce conflicting information. An example of this would be, "Are my keys in, under, behind or on top of my dresser?" **Your success will depend on your ability to develop clear, precise, specific, direct, orderly, chronological, step-by-step, layer-by-layer, near-to-far, in-to-the-out, top-to-bottom, big-to-small approach to your flow of questions.** There are many aspects to consider in developing the depth of your line of questioning. For example, sometimes it may be just as important to determine what *isn't* than what *is*. Sometimes measuring how much something needs to be *off* may be more significant than what is *on*. **Again the importance of this warrants repeating,** *your answers will be only as good as your questions, and learning how to flow your questions is the art of this skill.*

The other main key to your success will depend on your ability to keep yourself objective and detached from the outcome. Having objectivity is an easy thing to talk about and agree upon but not always easy to maintain.

Detachment, objectivity and neutrality is a mind set from which you can create because you are able to get out of your own way and let everything work by itself. Thinking "Oh, isn't this interesting", or, "It doesn't matter to me one way or another as to how this is going to turn out" is the correct mind set. This type of stance is a healthy approach to dowsing, especially when there may be even the most remote chance that you have some investment in the outcome.

It is important to know what areas of one's life experience may have charged emotional feelings around them thereby reducing one's objectivity and therefore one's accuracy. In other words, if you are doing your own work on an emotionally charged area of your life and it calls for a big decision or action of great consequence, it may be best to ask for assistance from multiple people who can check in and verify or clarify your answers.

Your mind needs to be in neutral and quiet, never letting thought or desire interfere with, or influence, the answers you seek. You can *not* have an opinion or feeling towards the question if you want accurate answers. Your feelings and desires will influence the swing of the pendulum. You must be aware of what your mind is doing at the time of the questioning. Any thoughts about a possible answer, any personal desire, wandering mind, any ego involvement or tendency to show off will influence your work. If you are grounded, centered and balanced, and you know that you are completely non-attached to the outcome with clear, specific, objective questions, you can trust in your intuitive answers. To attain a neutral state is perhaps the most difficult part of mastering the pendulum, but once attained will give you an invaluable tool for life. Neutrality requires an "I don't know" attitude. If for example, a condition was poor yesterday, it may be the same today, it may have improved or regressed. So, the approach is, "I really don't know."

Of course, timing, place, emotional and mental balance are also important variables. Always ask, "Is this the right time and/or the right place to be asking this question?", "Is this the appropriate question?", "To what ____(%) degree am I invested in the outcome?" and finally, "To what ____(%) degree do I have clear and total access to the Intuition?" If you receive a negative or a No answer, wait for another time or place, or go on to another question. By asking the question, "Is this the right time, place, or appropriate question?," you establish a trust and respect with your Intuition. The questions regarding percent of investment or access are extremely important questions that assist you in determining how much 'stock' to put in your results. If you have a 75% emotional investment in the outcome with a 45% clear access to the Intuition then it would certainly be advantageous for you to look at the subject another time or have someone else look at the subject for you. Do not be proud about needing help. Ask someone whom you know can stay in neutral to be of assistance. For example, suppose you have wanted to work with children for as long as you can remember. A job offer comes that would seem to fill this need. With an intense emotional agenda, it can be very difficult to assess whether or not this would be the job for you. When in doubt, after you have thoroughly checked it out with your Intuition, ask for help from a neutral pendulist for a second read.

The next step is to set the parameters or boundaries concerning your questions. In doing dowsing work for others we must **always** respect their private space and keep appropriate boundaries. We always need to be certain that we have permission to dowse from what we perceive as the Source of the Highest Good as well as from the person himself/herself. This is to make sure that we do not violate the space of the person in question. Remember that whenever we do dowsing that involves someone else, we will be entering that person's private space. Whether it is another individual, their property or land, it is imperative that we do not invade these private spaces, and so we follow a sequence of *May I, Can I, Should I* questions:

- *May I* seek this information—that is, am I permitted to do this?

- *Can I* receive a clear answer that will allow me to be of appropriate service—am I able, do I have the skill? Being good in one form of dowsing does not assure accurate results in another.

- *Should I* seek it— is it the appropriate time and am I the one to do it? It may be that a particular type of dowsing is appropriate for you to do at that particular time. Even with the right intention, one can still be inappropriate with the right answers at the wrong time.

We need to realize that there are some circumstances or situations which are intended to be as they are for reasons beyond our awareness or understanding. What may appear as a nasty or traumatic situation may prove to be a miracle in disguise later on. By dowsing to acquire permission, we are asking for awareness beyond our logical reason. Though we may not always understand why, we must learn to ask permission, and refuse to go farther if we get a negative response even when a friend client insists that they want us to do a session.

Asking the *right* question in the *right* way is 99% of the dowsing skill. If you do not know precisely what you are asking, the Intuition can *not* give you a correct response. Having knowledge of the subject helps immensely in knowing not only what to ask but how to be specific. Most often, the more information you have on the subject, the more you are able to be precise with your questions, and the greater potential for accuracy and success. (For further details regarding phrasing of questions, see the *Pendulum Charts* section.)

I have found a big difference between asking a question and making a declarative statement to the Intuition. I believe that the subconscious mind takes every word literally and a declarative statement becomes accepted as a "your wish is my command" response. I see the difference as, on one hand, asking a question from a fear based position in comparison to declaring from a place of strength, clarity, reverence and knowing.

Your quest for information will work best when you use questions or declarative statements. When using statements, you want to use a positive declarative format. For example:

Is now the best time to do this reading?

Is this the best place to do this?

My intuitive accuracy is what % today?

Is it to my highest and greatest benefit to _____ at this time, to what % _____?

This plant is in need of _____?

The lost object is what direction or degree from this point?

This body is in need of what remedy for this situation?

Again I would like to emphasize that it takes practice and time to gain confidence and develop your Intuitive skills. Start with some simple exercises and move on to more complex work. When you proceed to areas where you may be emotionally involved, you will find that you can trust your objectivity in these areas to a greater degree. However, when doing personal questioning where you have an investment in the outcome, again we strongly suggest that you see the answers as, "Oh, this is very interesting, but, we'll see." When you see the same answers coming up over and over, month after month, then you may add more validity to the acquired answers.

With knowledge comes power, and to have access to the Infinite Knowledge, Infinite

Intelligence, Infinite Wisdom greatly increases your responsibility. **Your ability to avoid the traps of the ego (for example, becoming enraptured by a sense of personal power) will be tested.** Such ego entrapments can be avoided by prefacing all of your pendulum work with an affirmation that asserts that you are dowsing for the greatest good for yourself and others. Then follow with the threefold permission.

- "Infinite, or Infinite Spirit, allow this work to be of the very highest and greatest benefit to me."

- "Infinite, or Infinite Spirit, allow this work to be for this person's _____ (name) _____ highest and greatest benefit."

- "Let this be of thy will, not my will."

- "I invoke the Light and Love within. I AM a clear and perfect channel. Love and Light are my guides."

- "From the Lord God of my soul, allow the truth of truths to prevail."

- Then ask the threefold permission:

"May I?"— Am I permitted to ask or do this?

"Can I?" — Am I able? Do I have the skill to do this?

"Should I?" — Is this the time? Am I the one to do it?

If you do not get permission for all three, DO NOT continue. You may try again at another time or place, or when you are in a different mental-emotional state of mind. Consider the possibility that you may not be meant to know something. For example, " Is it true that Aunt Milly is going to die today?" or "Is it true that they are going to lie to me?", "Is now the best time to get all the right Lottery numbers?" or "Is now the best time to find out if my friend's wife is cheating on him?" Most humans have such curious minds. It requires restraint in keeping appropriate boundaries. The best rule of thumb is, *don't go where you have not been invited.*

Subtle-Sensing

After some development of the dowsing skill, sensing the answers to your questions can often be experienced in more ways than movement of the pendulum. Veteran dowsers do not just see the answers in the movements of the pendulum, they also feel or sense the answers in terms of frequency registration in their hands, arms, or entire bodies. Some extremely clairsentient dowsers can feel a kind of contact and the presence of information in answer to their question(s) through a sudden subtle sensation of an itch, tingle, change in body temperature, ringing in the ear, feeling of nausea pressure, discomfort (associated with solar plexus responses) and, in some cases, dizziness. These types of sensations can be incredibly accurate in letting you know, through physical response, the answer to your line of questioning or a caution of something that may occur.

The process of both dowsing and subtle-sensing are the same. The subconscious and conscious mind receives and interprets the information from the Intuition through feelings and impressions. This information is then passed on through the dowser's sympathetic and parasympathetic nervous system down to micro-movement of the muscles in the hand or fingers. The dowser may be attuned to not only the pendulum movements which seem independent of conscious physical control, but he/she may also be aware of subtle-sensing that is experienced in other parts of the body. This, like your pendulum language, can be in addition to your expanded communication form. For further development and application of subtle-sensing see KNOWING Your Intuitive Mind by Dale Olson.

New Communication

In your pendulum work, you may find sooner or later that your existing pendulum language may be inadequate for handling a particular problem or application. You may find yourself needing to improvise. It may be a new experience or an improved procedure meeting the often unexpected dowsing need of the moment. It is a matter of responding to spontaneous inclination to use a new pendulum pattern that may access additional information. For example, you may be locating something and know you are near the object of your quest, and suddenly find your pendulum behaving in a new and unexpected way; attempting for example, to make a figure 8 or rotating in a right or left oval. What does it mean? Is the subconscious mind trying to tell you something beyond the range of your present pendulum language? Take the time to meditate upon its meaning. See if you can sense an impression or visualize an image on your mental screen, or feel a truth in the body, or hear something new. You can develop new additions to pendulum language by working through and expanding on programs of this nature. These new pendulum movements are the result of the Intuition improvising in order to show you another or new way to measure something. They are in addition to one's established pendulum language. Once your pendulum language is established, it should never be altered. Once it has been ingrained into the subconscious mind, you may expand upon it, but not be changed. For thousands of years the master teachers have emphasized the foolishness of attempting to change positive symbolic forms that have meanings entrenched in the matrix of the unconscious or subconscious mind.

Mind Preparation

Approach the pendulum with *enthusiasm and confidence* that you are able to use it, because a halfhearted or doubtful attitude will only result in uncertain findings. Always work, if possible, in quiet surroundings by yourself, away from skeptics, negative thoughts, or anyone trying to influence you. See yourself, the operator, as a supersensitive receiver. This will help in your development.

Because we live in less then a positive, harmonious, and secure world, I feel that all work of this nature needs to be surrounded by some kind of shielding. I believe that the *White Light and Love* is the Source, the God lifeforce that dwells in all things. To make this protective shielding, visualize yourself enveloped by the *White Light & Love*. Take a *White Light & Love* shower. Visualize yourself drawing in the *White Light & Love* through the bottom of your feet; let it go up your legs, up your spine, up and out through the top of your head, and then let it shower down all around you. Maintain this glow of protective *White Light & Love*, and feel the unconditional love throughout your being. This universal method of shielding oneself from psychic intrusion has been used throughout the ages to protect oneself and others from outside influences. This technique or one that you feel will be as protective, along with some of the starting affirmations and the threefold permission, will greatly assist you in keeping a protective field around you and others with whom you may be working. It also is imperative to maintain a balanced mental-emotional mind.

Self-conditioning is essential for successful dowsing and other intuitive work. Before you go to work on a project, we suggest that you spend several minutes doing the *White Light & Love* shower and self-conditioning. Then, for example, if I were dowsing for gold, I would go through all of the steps within my imagination. I would visualize the dowsing process step by step through to the actual digging and the finding of the gold.

Practice makes perfect. I work on self-conditioning every day. I mentally go over each project or task in my mind. It is easier for most to visualize a step-by-step project than to see some of the more intangible tasks that we often present to the Intuition. In applying this technique to the construction business, I saw that for every hour I visualized in this way I saved three or more hours of work on the job site with less error and therefore greater success.

To take this technique one step further using the locating of the gold example, I take the time to prepare my mind before going out on a site. I visualize a mental tour of of the land. I first establish an arbitrary starting point (tree, rock formation) in relationship to the lay of the land. I then look around for the minerals. I pretend I am looking into the earth and searching for the gold-bearing ore. When I spot the ore, I make a mental note of its location in relationship to the earth's surface. I then complete my mental experience by visualizing the ore being successfully brought to the earth's surface. Most often, when I visit the site, the land will look exactly as I had visualized, and the ore is sometimes located in the spot that I had mentally envisioned. This basic technique can be used in just about any application that you can imagine.

Another example would be in finding a location for a water well. Mentally standing at the front door of the house I would ask: "In what direction is the best place for a well?" , "What is the flow and direction of the water?", "What is the quality of the water?" and so forth.

Imagination and visualization are extremely powerful tools, and among the most important disciplines taught in all shamanic training. To successfully visualize, the mind needs to be relaxed, balanced, and quiet. Shamans often used peyote, jimson weed and other hallucinogenic plants to induce flights of imagination and to open the way to the inner self. I do not advocate the use of drugs in any way for I believe that controlled breathing can produce similar results in a more controlled and beneficial fashion (see the section on Mastery of the Breath).

Developing and directing your guided imagery will not only assist you in successful dowsing applications, it will also help you to explore the limitless inner resources of your own consciousness.

All of these pendulum functions point to scientific and measurable methods of accessing the Intuition. In order to achieve these higher levels, you must get through the basics of form and the clearing of ego responses. The next chapter will introduce these aspects and attributes.

Chapter 4

Emotional and Mental Interference

There are basics in any skill which must be learned and practiced, and dowsing is sometimes seemingly more art than science. The skills you need are important. What happens when an individual doesn't learn dowsing basics? First of all, we have seen individuals who learn some dowsing skills and if they do not immediately get accurate results, they stop using the pendulum and tell their friends that it doesn't work. Secondly, we have seen dowsing receive criticism as the result of people who, after having been shown how to dowse, pick up a pendulum or dowsing rods and find they can indeed get a dowsing response. Immediately claiming to be experts, they go out and tell their friends to dig here and drill there..... and chaos results.

By learning and practicing the basics, it is possible to become a successful dowser. A stumbling block in the development of dowsing skills, and in the development of the communication between self and the Intuition, is mental or emotional interference. It is the one thing that eats at the very core of one's trust, and without trust you have nothing. Practice will help develop trust. Additional stumbling blocks which may prevent successful intuitive dowsing include:

- Trivial use of the pendulum

47

- Fortune-telling, predicting the future

- Impatience, fatigue

- Mental distractions, overconfidence

- Undue influence from skeptics

- Lack of concentration

- Needless superstition or limiting beliefs

- Poorly defined communication or language between the conscious and the Intuition.

- Imperfect coordination between one's mind and the instrument

- Imbalanced emotional state of mind: fears, doubts, anger, resentments, sadness, grief, anxiety, greed, jealousy...

Certainly, the pendulum is a remarkable tool that allows us to reach out for answers that are beyond our ordinary intellectual scope. Because the intuitive ability is so extraordinary, it is best not to use it for trivial or minor matters. For example: "Should I have the green salad or the spinach salad for lunch?" or, "Should I use a blue pen or black pen to write this letter?" These may seem farfetched examples, but I think we all know people who do ask similar petty questions. If you misuse your intuitive abilities in the way that many people have misused the Ouija board and other forms of divination, you will be using the pendulum at the level of a parlor game.

If you are trying to find out when you are going to die, when you will find the person of your dreams, or when you will win the lottery, and other types of fortune-telling, it safe to say that you may find yourself greatly disappointed. If you merely play with the pendulum as if it were a game, the results will be superficial and you will only get what is in your own subconscious and mental mind, and not information from your Intuition or the collective consciousness. By collective consciousness I mean all the information that is available from the universe; all thought, thought forms both manifested and unmanifested. If you use the same clearing, balancing and centering techniques with your mind for more common daily decision-making, and go into that slightly diffused or altered state of consciousness, you will always have a better probability of accessing information that will assist you to make better daily choices in decision-making, and it will also develop your intuitive proficiency.

One area of dowsing that many find to be tempting is predicting the future. Even if you have many years of successful, accurate dowsing, it is best to avoid the area of predicting the future altogether. It does not mean that you can't look at a line of continuity if all present variables were kept constant. By this we mean, looking at a subject that has a certain history with "X" variables, conditions and responses that is then carried in a time line into the future and the potential outcome is measured. For example, if I were measuring the potential outcome from applying a particular type of therapy to an injury on my body and I wanted to know what the potential well-being factor will be in "X" amount of time, I would ask the following: "Infinite, if all present variables were to be kept constant, and I was to apply only _____ therapy to this injury, my probability for total healing or well-being would be in _____(%) in _____ days, weeks, months..... etc." This way I could compare the potential for various forms of therapy and perhaps a combination of therapies. I could then discern the potential of what course of action would be most beneficial for me. When used properly, the Intuition tunes into the universal consciousness where the Infinite Intelligence will bring forth the appropriate information. Those who work at predicting the future in other ways know that time element are the most difficult to forecast. The only time the pendulum, or Intuition can tell you something regarding the immediate future is when the information is already present in the human consciousness. You cannot get an accurate reading before people have made up their minds about an event or outcome. In order for it to be available to you, the information must be factual and exist somewhere in the collective consciousness, at which point it can be brought through the Intuition and then to the conscious mind.

Sometimes individuals using the pendulum complain of unexpected confusion, lack of consistent agreement with oneself, alternating *Yes* and *No* answers, erratic responses of the instrument, and outright failure. This is sometimes followed by temporary or partial loss of one's dowsing ability. This type of problem mostly occurs from impatience, fatigue, mental distractions, emotional upset, overconfidence, or undue influence from skeptics.

Superstition can limit your dowsing ability. Believing that magical formulas, including dowsing at a particular time of day, a certain place, only under certain weather conditions, or while you are wearing certain types of clothes, etc., are the *only* way your intuitive abilities will function means you have sold yourself a program. Once you have set such a limitation in dowsing, you will be stuck with it until you examine and release the program.

Some people believe that dowsing is a gift bestowed only on them and a precious few. These people are on an "ego trip." This belief is an outright fallacy and simply another limitation. Some people do learn more quickly when adopting these skills, however, most skilled dowsers have withstood the tests of time and patience, and most admit that dowsing finesse is usually acquired through some tribulations of trial-and-error as well as continued practice.

Successful Dowsing Form

- Communication: Is this the right question, at the right time, at the right place

- Balance: Mental and emotional balance, a relaxed state of mind

- Breathing techniques

- Meditation, Prayer, Affirmation

- Practice, Patience, Persistence

- TRUST in yourself and the source of your Intuition

Once again, we emphasize the necessity of *affirmation, prayers, shielding* (the *White Light* shower), and asking for the *threefold permission* before doing your pendulum dowsing. Remember that it is good practice to preface your intuitive work with a starting affirmation or prayer such as; "Open the way for that which is of the highest and greatest benefit," or "Let this be of Thy will and not my will," or, "Let this be for my highest and greatest benefit," or, "Let the truth of truths prevail from the Lord God of my Soul," or, "I invoke the Christ within, I Am a clear and perfect channel, Love and Light is my guide." Find an affirmation or prayer that works for you and your belief system. Affirmations, prayer, the *White light* shower, and the *threefold permission* are extremely powerful in offsetting the interference of the ego, the intellect, and outside influence.

Dowsing embraces the implicit belief that we do what we do through love—for the greatest good of all concerned. This means dowsers must realize what to do with the answers they receive through their Intuition. As discussed earlier not all knowledge that we discover through dowsing is appropriate to pass on. We must look to our moral code in regard to boundaries and let our Intuition assist us in determining what is appropriate to check and what to share. I have always found the Intuition to access not only infinite knowledge but also the wisdom to use it properly. So be it!

Chapter 5

Self Mastery

I Now Breathe In Life Fully.
I Relax and Trust The Process of Life.

Mastery of the Breath

Practicing affirmations, prayer, *threefold permission,* and the *White light* shower will go a long way to insure that your pendulum work is clear, objective, and for the greatest benefit of all concerned. Mastering breathing skills will assist you in being emotionally and mentally balanced. Practicing certain breathing techniques can be invaluable to clear negativity from within or from outside of you and help to promote a state of well-being.

By emotional balance I mean a state of emotional harmony, neutral feelings neither too high nor too low, but centered. This means your thoughts need to be in neutral without attachment to the outcome, and without any critical or judgmental thoughts toward yourself or others. Fears, doubts, anger, resentment, greed, anxiety, jealousy, etc. can be the greatest hindrances to the development of the Intuition (as they can be hindrances in all aspects of life).

Of course, we already know that it is imperative to be free of negative emotions if we want high quality living. Packing these feelings around is not what we would call a good time. But most of us have never been taught very effective ways of neutralizing or transforming this negative "stuff." We can release negative mental and emotional thoughts and feelings with the following breath techniques. Many of us have had years, or even a lifetime, of poor breathing habits. These poor breathing habits, most often are responsible for many of our imbalanced or negative states. Have you ever noticed, when someone becomes fearful he or she will almost stop breathing and basically "shuts off." In my therapy practice I have seen hundreds of individuals who shut down their breathing when feeling "not good enough" or, "when fearing failure" or, "not going to get what I want" and many more. This dynamic is quite destructive because it creates a vicious circle of poor breathing habits and patterns of negativity. Breathing mastery is one of the most beneficial skills that one can acquire. It is a way to heal all aspects of one's life.

I feel that this section is *the* most important part of this entire book. Much credit goes to Dr. Marcel Vogel, Paramahansa Yogananda, Yogi Ramacharaka, and many other authors, researchers and teachers who know and teach that the breath is the key to mental and emotional balance, optimal health, and well-being. The techniques that follow are extremely dynamic. Practice and experience them firsthand to realize the incredible power and healing potential available to you.

In all of the breathing techniques I will share, there are several parts on which to focus. First of all, you will want to create a neutral place in your mind and your *intention*. *Intend* for your work to reflect the principle "for your highest and greatest good." Secondly, let your ego go; trust your Intuition. Lastly, relax into the breathing technique which you are practicing. (Learn it well so that you can call upon it at any time.)

This will take some practice, so be patient, willing, and enthusiastic. Remember, it *is* a learning process.

In summary, mastery of the breath is the key:

- To help heal all aspects of the physical, mental, and emotional self.

- To balance the emotional-mental mind.

- To oxygenate the cells of the body.

- To draw in Prana (universal life force).

- To release the power of thought.

- To release stress and promote relaxation.

- To neutralize negative and critical thought forms.

- To release old imprints and assist in restoring one's personal power.

- To release fears, doubts, anger, resentment, greed, grief, jealousy.

- To open intuitive channels.

- To create protective psychic shields.

When we breathe deeply, we invigorate the entire body through oxygenation of the cells, and we bring in the vital charge of energy called Prana, which is the universal life force. This vital force sends its currents through all body systems and is absorbed down to the individual cells of the body. Your degree of health and vitality is determined by your ability to absorb and circulate Prana. When you inhale deeply, you pull more Prana into your body. Prana is utilized by the mind to build the patterns of thought, being, and intention of what we wish to do, be, or perform. Our intention comes on the indwelling breath. Inhalation draws an electrical charge into the body (negative electrical charge); exhalation discharges an opposite polarity (positive electrical charge). Inhalation draws Prana (life force) in, and exhalation releases the power of thought. We express our thoughts with each exhalation. If you don't believe this, try carrying on a conversation while only inhaling.

First Breath Technique for Emotional and Mental Balance

The first technique is used to bring about balance of the emotional and mental mind. This is accomplished by utilizing the dynamics of the breathing mechanism itself. This technique can be used for releasing accumulated negativity, relaxing, and mental clarity.

To use the breath in this first release method:

- Create the intention in your mind to be in a clear, positive and a harmonious state of mind. Intend to free yourself from any negative or critical thoughts.

- Breathe *in* through your *nose* with this intention and create an image in your mind of yourself in this balanced state. How do you appear, how do you feel while in this state?

- Breathe *out* through your *mouth* slowly and easily, releasing any and all negative thoughts or patterns. It is best not to forcefully exhale, but ever-so-slowly release these negative and critical thoughts with blessings, rather than with anger.

- Continue to breathe *in* through your *nose*, imprinting positive patterns of thoughts or affirmations toward yourself or others. Breathe *out* through your *mouth* any negative imprints, patterns, or thoughts. Do this release and balancing exercise, breathing in and out in a connected loop; breathe deeply, evenly, and completely.

This kind of breathing technique can take anywhere from five minutes to half-an-hour to bring the body and mind to a harmonious state of clarity and balance. Again, release negative patterns of thought by breathing out through the mouth. Imprint positive patterns of thought by breathing in through the nose with intention, positive thoughts and affirmations.

Second Breath Technique for Balancing and Meditation

To use the second technique:

- Start by sitting with your back straight (you can sit in a chair or on the floor—it makes no difference).

- Begin to breathe in and out through your nose slowly, deeply, connecting the breath.

- While you're doing this circular breathing, connecting the inhalation and the exhalation, visualize the energy in your spine going up and down like a thermometer with red mercury. With each breath in, the red mercury goes up the thermometer. With each breath out, the red mercury goes down the thermometer.

Do this connected breath only 14 times, as suggested by Paramahansa Yogananda. This technique works best if done twice a day (in the morning and evening) to assist you in maintaining a positive, meditative state. Of course, this exercise can be done at any time to bring you into mental or emotional balance, to initiate meditation, or to create a state conducive for working with your Intuition.

Micro & Pulsed Breath

The next breath techniques have been labeled the Micro and Pulsed Breath. They came into form through Marcel Vogel as the result of his research with adept Yogi masters from India. The material that is to follow is a shortened version; it will take only a few hours of practice to start feeling the empowering affects. Some masters have spent many, many years practicing these techniques in order to acquire the total dynamic results. Of course, you are getting a scaled-down version. It is, nonetheless, extremely beneficial as well as powerful. These invaluable breath techniques are now yours if you choose to learn, practice and develop them.

In the first stage in mastery of the breath, we learn how to maintain a holding pattern at the upward stroke of the indwelling breath.

58

By holding the breath at the completion of the indwelling breath, we create *Pranayama*. Pranayama is a term that describes the opening of all psychic faculties— "all channels open." Historically, this was seen as the ability to see through the "Third Eye" ("Brow Chakra" or "Ajna Center"). Holding the breath at this point is imperative because it allows for both the transference of oxygen and also, the formation of the intent of that which you desire (to do, be, or experience.) Holding your breath allows your intended thought to permeate your body. This completes this part of the process.

This "holding" of the breath is not "holding" as we are accustomed. It is *not* forced. Instead, it is the slightest breath taken in the uppermost part of your lungs. You will be breathing so slightly that if someone were observing you, they would think that you were not breathing at all. This ever-so-slight breath is called the *Micro-Breath*. This is the type of breathing that the yogis do in a deep state of meditation where they appear not to be breathing and are beyond the feeling of physical pain, beyond the physical realm with all of their psychic channels open. It is not something that takes a lifetime to learn. However, it does take some time and a good deal of practice. The first thing to learn is that doing the *Micro-Breath* will not cause a deficiency of oxygen. There is no need to fear not having enough oxygen. This is usually the first fear you will need to overcome. Again, it is not a matter of holding your breath; you will be able to maintain all body functions just fine. This technique of breathing will probably feel strange at first; it is just a matter of getting used to this ever-so-slight breathing.

Micro-Breath Technique

- Sit or stand comfortably with your spine perfectly straight.

- Fill your lungs completely as you inhale.

- As you breathe in, imagine that you are drawing in with your breath large amounts of prana and circulating this energy through all parts of your body.

- Now, let out 1/4 of your breath and begin to maintain the *Micro-Breath*.

- Your lungs will remain expanded, back straight, diaphragm in the upward position in your rib cage, rib cage completely expanded, and an ever-so-slight breath going slowly in and out of your lungs.

- You are not conscious of exhaling, for the air just seems to go out without noticeable movement of the lungs; it is a sensation of drawing air in on almost a continuous basis.

- You can also sense a slight movement at the top of the lungs and sometimes a coolness in the bronchial part of the lungs. Do the *Micro-Breath* again, and this time maintain it for as long as possible and feel this ever-so-slight in-and-out movement, even though your rib cage is fully expanded.

Many people can maintain the *Micro Breath* for as long as 20 minutes or more, and the yogis can do this type of *Micro-Breath* for hours. Now, try the *Micro-Breath* again, and this time with your eyes closed, focus your perception through your Third Eye (or Ajna center), which is at the center of your forehead. What did you see? Light? When you maintain the *Micro-Breath* your alpha brainwaves greatly increase, and all of your psychic capacities or channels begin to open. Again, this state is called *Pranayama,* whereby one is able to see through the Third Eye, Brow Chakra, or Ajna Center. Often, this sight is manifested in the ability to see light through the Third Eye. If this state is maintained long enough, you can have an out-of-body experience. The Kundalini also opens with the *Micro-Breath.* Kundalini is the life force or prana which comes in from the top of the head, and with the breath, goes down to the bottom of the spine in a rhythmic pumping action. When this energy hits the bottom of the spine (or base chakra), it spins up in waves in a form of a double helix (☿ Caduceus). This double helix of energy spins up and down generating an electrical field. When you draw in your breath you start the generation of this energy, and the *Micro-Breath* (holding on the indwelling breath) builds the magnitude of the electrical energy. This is what is called "raising the Kundalini."

The Pulsed Breath

The *Pulsed Breath* is used for instant balancing and centering. It will bring equilibrium to our mental, emotional, and physical bodies for neutralizing negative or critical thoughts or patterns. Too much positive energy, such as anticipation or over excitement, can also create imbalance which can be balanced with the pulsed breath. The *Pulsed Breath* is the carrier wave for our thoughts and the intentions behind them. To do the pulsed breath:
• Draw in the breath holding the intention of that which you want to do, be or perform.

61

- Hold the breath on the upward stroke of the indwelling breath, doing the *Micro-Breath*. Focus your energy from the Heart and Brow energy centers of your body, into your intention (that which you wish to do, be, or perform).

- When you have reached the level of the greatest magnitude (or critical mass) the breath is quickly released through the nostrils with a strong expulsion and a snapping-type contraction of the abdominal muscles and diaphragm. The *Pulsed Breath* will sound and appear like a strong snort out through the nose.

- With practice, the power of the *Pulsed Breath* increases and you will feel the difference.

Clearing and Balancing Technique

Using both the *Micro* and *Pulsed Breath*.

This is a technique to clear negativity, bring yourself to balance, and clear the ego-intellect out of the way in order to prepare for intuitive questioning.

This technique is especially useful if you have been exposed to intense negative energy or if you feel out of balance.

To Clear:

- Draw in the breath with your intention to clear. Visualize love and light surrounding you.

- Maintain the *Micro-Breath*, build the energy level to critical mass; see the light building around your intention. Build up the energy, build it , build it and then......

- Do the *Pulsed-Breath*. See and feel the negative energy shatter. Feel your energy field and state of mind instantly shift to a state of mental and emotional balance. Now, you are ready to go about your day or to begin the work with the Intuition.

The Intuition works effortlessly. A relaxed state of mind is essential for effective pendulum work, and the breath is the key for a balanced state of your mind. You will become more conscious of your breath. With continued practice and deeper and more meaningful breathing, you will experience more energy, vitality, and greater clarity of mind. The breath awareness techniques in this chapter will assimilate into your daily experience if you practice them regularly. By using these techniques to clear negative patterns, and by replacing those negative patterns with affirmations and focused intent, you will increase your quality of living. The breath is the key which unlocks the door to Self Mastery and well-being.

Chapter 6

Pendulum Applications

We can use our Intuition to assist us in unlimited ways for everyday decision-making and intuitive problem-solving. We can use our intuitive tools to:

Choose: the right foods, diet, vitamins, minerals, supplements, crystals, books, remedies, careers, teachers, doctors, employees, employers, locations to live, the right house or car...

Find: the right job, lost objects, missing people or pets, buried treasure, underground water, gas, or electrical lines, valuables, underground water, springs, minerals, ore mines, metals, oil, directions, schools of fish, ruins, graves, old monuments and buried artifacts, tunnels, geo-energy (magnetic) lines...

Discover: potential relationship compatibility of partners, friends, potential employees or employers, personal motivators, what is going on, where to from here, who is involved, what am I telling myself, probability of success for any situation...

Make: accurate business decisions, best consumer choices, career moves...

Determine: probable sex of unborn children or animals, plant needs and soil deficiencies, diagnostics for repairs of your house or automobile, weather conditions, written or printed errors, positioning antennae, whether foods are sprayed with pesticides or irradiated, whether foods are organic or nonorganic...

Test: seeds, soil, and potential planting areas, purity and quality of food and liquids, authenticity of signatures, nutritional value...

Analyze: physical, mental, emotional, or etheric body of either yourself or others, including all needs, deficiencies, imbalances, patterns, fears, or blockages.

We really *do* have access to what we call the Infinite Intelligence and the collective consciousness! This allows us access to the knowledge of not only our own innate wisdom, but also the collective consciousness of all humankind. With development, we do have the ability to access information and to find answers to almost any questions that we can imagine.

Again, the pendulum acts as the means to make what is already know by our Intuition available to our conscious mind. The pendulum has been used by people throughout history to determine an infinite amount of information and knowledge that had been considered *unknown.*

Everyone is a "natural" dowser, but some people have to suspend their innate disbelief before they can claim and develop this inherent intuitive ability. Regardless of some past beliefs or what others may think, continue your practice and be determined that you will be successful. If you get a response that is not precise, be patient; remember that you are still a student. Mistakes can go a long way to assist you in refining your pendulum skills. Remind yourself of the nature and specifics of the pendulum language and make the effort to understand why you may have received an inaccurate response. Look to the effect, then trace it backwards to the cause. The problem you are facing is not about your ability to dowse, it is about the refinement and clarity of the questions you formulate and the image you hold, as well as being in neutral as you go through the dowsing process.

Finding Direction Method

Follow the subsequent instructions to find the direction for: land, water, lost object or a person, buried treasure, ruins.

• Stand erect with your pendulum suspended in the neutral, or search position, about 12 inches directly in front of your chest with your elbow tucked against your side, Watch the pendulum out of your peripheral vision for any changes in the direction of the swing.

• Be prepared to turn your body clockwise in a complete 360 degree circle.

• Begin the swing of your pendulum in a sideways motion.

• Fix the object or substance of your search firmly in your mind. Repeat it over and over, if necessary, to keep your focus.

• With your left arm stretched out, point with your left hand or finger.

- Slowly begin pivoting your body clockwise (right), repeating in your mind, "The object of this search can be found directly in line with my pointing left finger: *Yes/No/Maybe?*"

- Slowly continue your turn, repeat your question often, until you notice a deviation in the swing. This is a change from a sideways oscillation, to a maybe, greater-or-lesser position, and then into the forward-and-backward (or Yes) swing.

- When you are positive of the change, inscribe a line in the dirt with your foot or place a marker (a piece of wood, stone etc.) in alignment with the determined direction.

- Repeat this process as you slowly continue turning your body clockwise until you return to the beginning point. Throughout the search you may find one or more changes in the swing of your pendulum. It is possible to have two or more *find points*. This may be somewhat confusing. This may be due to a distraction, mind wandering, or in reality, there could be two find points. There are other possibilities that could be connected to your search in some way that could give you an indication of a *find point*. A piece of information or a fragment of the lost, buried, hidden object, though of secondary importance, can cause your pendulum to respond.

- To double-check your findings, return to your starting point. Now slowly pivoting your body counterclockwise, repeat all the steps. Observe the pendulum's swing. Check to see if the pendulum's motion shift corresponds to your earlier clockwise pivot. If you still get confused answers and feel uncertain about the direction of the *find points*, begin again with the first step and repeat the procedure. Keep your attention focused on the objective of your questioning. Resist being distracted by physical movements and surrounding visual stimuli. Take a break if you need to.

• To double-check your answer(s), align yourself with the directional marker(s), swing your pendulum in a search mode for a *Yes* or *No* response, with the statement, "The object or substance of this search can be found in this direction." If you receive a *Yes* answer you may proceed with confidence in the direction of the object or substance of your search.

With practice, the coordination of your pendulum and body movements will become easier, and finally, automatic. You can, with practice, master the technique of finding direction.

At this point you have learned to determine the specific direction(s) that will lead you to the *find point* of the object or substance of the search. Since you don't have a map where "X" marks the spot, the next step in your development is to be able to locate the *find point*.

Locating Find Points

You have determined the direction(s) of the substance or object of your search. To locate your *find point*:

• Walk forward slowly with your pendulum swinging side-to-side. Repeat the question in your mind... "The *object* of my search can be found here?" Your pendulum language in this procedure calls for the instrument to change from the side-to-side (or *No*) swing to a *Maybe* swing position as you come into the vicinity of the *find point,* and then into a forward-and-backward (or *Yes*) swing at the immediate edge or point of contact with the object or substance of the search. The change in swing will occur regardless of whether the object is overhead or underground, moving or stationary, disguised, mixed, fragmented, or scattered.

- The instant your pendulum makes a change in swing, mark the spot. You are most likely at the *find point.* Some caution needs to be exerted. If you are walking too fast, you may not have given your pendulum enough time to alter its movement. If this is true, you may have walked several steps beyond the starting perimeter(s) of the object, or substance, of your inquiry.

- You have now located the *find point.* If the perimeters of the object of your search are vague, (for example, an underground stream or mineral vein), you have found the boundary of one side. If this is the case, mark the edge of the object and walk several yards across it, turn around and approach the object from the opposite direction using the same method previously described.

- Repeat these steps from all directions, or from enough points, until you have a general outline of the *find point* area.

- To mark the edge of the complete perimeters of your underground stream, pipeline or cache, walk slowly, inscribing a line in the earth with a stick trailing beside you. Watch for any deviation of your pendulum's forward-and-backward swing. If the line is curving in its form, make notes of the arc or change in course as you follow it back to the starting point. If you start getting weak or erratic pendulum movement, it may be that you are getting off-track. Lay the stick down in line with the direction last noted; then, walk several steps away from, or perpendicular to, your marker. Now approach the stick (object's perimeters) and watch for any change in swing of your pendulum. At the point of a *Yes* swing, you are once again on the true edge of the object's perimeters where you may resume your edge marking to completion.

Defining Depth

Now that you have learned to find direction and determine the *find point* or perimeters of a location, defining depth of the object or substance is the next variable to establish. If your particular application requires measurement distance down or up to your *find point*, use your counting language, swinging your pendulum in the side-to-side (or *No*) motion. Ask for the depth to be indicated in inches, feet, yards or miles to the "top" of the object of the search. You can learn about the object's height by repeating your depth measurement, but this time, ask to gauge the bottom depth of the object or substance. When you are searching for underground water, mineral veins, etc., there are often additional streams, pools, or veins located below or next to the original *find point*. It is to your advantage to assess the area thoroughly to be certain that you are at the original *find point* before moving on.

Pendulum Applications

WATER

Finding pure water is becoming a very important issue, and it will become more so as time goes on.

The world community suffers from a lack of sufficient, unpolluted water. The water supply in the U.S. is polluted by toxic chemicals from agricultural runoff, manufacturing by-products, and deliberate chemical pollution. In rural America, some 15 million people suffer from a daily dose of unclean drinking water. Over 30 million Americans lack decent sanitation. In the developing world, 16,000 children under the age of five years of age die EACH DAY from water-related diseases. On a global basis, 30,000 deaths are reported daily as a result of water-related diseases. Dowsing can assist in the search for pure water, and can determine the degree of purity in any potable water.

Many beginning dowsing books encourage people to attempt to become instant dowsing experts. We do not want to give anyone the impression that dowsing for water is easy and that anyone can do it. Dowsing for water is an art that each person seems to possess to varying degrees. It takes *practice* to reach your potential, *and* there are some who seem to be born with this talent. All in all we highly suggest that you spend some time in training with a competent water dowser before going out and predicting for others where a water well should be driven.

Finding pure water can seem complicated, and often there is more to it than meets the eye. Like any other application, it is a matter of knowing how to ask the right questions. When a dowser requests potable water, he is requesting, by definition, water fit to drink. However, water fit to drink is not always beneficial. For instance, iron-rich water can be of value to those people who suffer from anemia, but it promotes cancer cell growth in cancer victims. Municipal water supplies are fit to drink, but many believe that chlorine converts to the carcinogenic chloroform.

As we dowse to determine well sites, we should also be asking for long-range health benefits from the potential water wells. Some other important questions to be asking are, "Will the water well be pure two hours from now, two days from now, two weeks from now?"

Testing Water: To test water for purity, form the statement in your mind of the object of this test: "Infinite, indicate if this water is for my highest and greatest benefit." Hold the pendulum over a cup of water; if it gyrates positively (clockwise) the water is fit to drink. Counterclockwise indicates that the water is in some way polluted and not fit to drink.

The second part of the test is forming the question, "Infinite, to what degree is this water pure?" Start out with a side-to-side or *Maybe* swing with your pendulum and begin the counting language while thinking in terms of percentage. For example; 10, 20, 30, 40, 50, 60, 70, 80, 90 and the pendulum swing goes to the *Yes* position. Keep going to 100 and it begins to deviate back to *Maybe*.

Water emerging from deep within the earth
forming domes, or pockets of water that
spread out into streams, or veins. The veins
radiating outward from the water dome are
the objective find point for a potential well
site. Sometimes these veins may reach the
surface as pure spring water.

Go back to 90, and continue counting 91, 92, 93, 94 and
again the swing starts to move toward the *Maybe* position,
return to 93. In this case 93% is the purity level of the
water.

Try this now on your own tap or well water, then compare it to a variety of brand bottled water. Currently there are very few regulations on bottled water, and simply because it's bottled water does not mean it's pure. We suggest that you even check out the differences between the bottled waters as to the percentage of purity.

Water Purity Test: Test a row of a dozen cups of water. Mix 1 teaspoon of salt into one cup. Now have someone mix the cups up so that the one containing the salt is unknown even to you the tester. Check each cup for it's percentage of purity. This is a good test to assist in the development of accuracy. If you have trouble choosing the correct one that does not mean that you can't do it, it just means that you need more practice.

Finding Water Practice

Water Finding Test 1:

It is good practice to start by tracking the direction of an existing buried water line. Practice at various sites detecting the buried water line and at what depth the pipe is lying. You can check your results by digging with a shovel, but go carefully so as to prevent breaking the water line.

Now that you know how to find a water pipe, know that it is very similar to finding potential water domes, except that now you're looking for a *natural* flow of water beneath your feet. There are little trickles of water everywhere underground, however, we want more than that; we are looking for a water flow, streams, pockets and water domes.

Water Finding Test 2:

Practice on an already established well site and learn to feel the water dome and it's parameters.

- Hold an actual sample of pure local spring water or well water from the well of this test and image what you're looking for.

- Start at least 200 or more feet back from the existing well.

- Allow your pendulum to swing in a side-to-side motion and slowly walk toward the edge of where you *feel* the water dome may be while holding the *image* of finding water firmly in mind.

- As you get closer to the stream of water or water dome, the pendulum will begin to swing to the *Maybe* (or more-or-less) position, and this may turn into a clockwise oval gyration. When you have reached the edge of the water dome or are directly over the search object, the pendulum movement will change to a full clockwise circle.

- If you continue beyond the stream *find point*, the pendulum will deviate back to an oval and eventually return to a side-to-side or *No* position.

Since you are making up the rules of communication here, you determine at what distance you want to be from the *find point* when the oval motion begins or ends, and then integrate that response as part of your pendulum language. Whatever response you develop, *you are the one in control*, so that any other response that is not part of your pendulum language may indicate either a random error, a distraction, or a clue that there is more involved than what you are seeing. If you experience conflicting results, repeat the test or try again at another time.

Throughout this series of tests for finding water, have you been noticing the differences in how everything *feels*? Did you notice any difference between how the water in the pipe and the water flow beneath your feet felt? There usually is a very large difference in *feel* between the two. If you didn't feel any real difference between the two, it doesn't mean that you were not successful, it only means that you may need more practice with learning to sense these subtle differences.

Water Volume/Flow Test 3:

- Using the water pipe technique, check the water flow in the pipe when the tap is open and gauge how that *feels*. Compare your results with past records of physical water volume/flow test in gallons per minute/hour. Now compare how it feels when the valve is closed. You should get a result of zero flow.

- Using the well site of Test 2, use your pendulum to measure the flow, the amount of water available over time in gallons per minute/per hour using the counting method. What difference in results do you get if you hold the image of the flow during different times of the year throughout a 10 or 20 year time span? Do your results change?

Calibrating the Mind with the Intuition

Sometimes we have to coordinate or calibrate our measurement scale between what the mental mind sees and what the Intuition is sensing. Sometimes what may be seen as equal one inch/gallon/mile may be sensed as 3 inches/gallons/mile. To calibrate between the two is easy. Go back to some of your original test in finding buried water lines or go to some new testing areas and check with your pendulum how deeply the water pipe is buried. If you get that the pipe is buried at 16" and it really is at 22" then you have found your "margin of difference" to be 6" every 16 inches. Practice this exercise until you have the actual difference between your mind and the Intuition coordinated. Sometimes, it may just be getting the space/time measurement coordinated. It may also be that the subconscious or conscious mind is more, optimistic, lets say by 10% more than what the physical reality may indicate. Usually these types of results are due to being attached to the outcome or some other mental-emotional interference.

In summary, there are a few variables in finding water that are all dependent on each other in finding a successful well site: location, depth, consistency of quantity and purity. Some people seem to have a natural affinity for finding water, but most often, it requires a great deal of practice, reading and/or learning from a master water dowser.

If you have developed your water dowsing ability and would like to assist in this critical world problem, contact the Global Water for Life organization in Washington, D.C.

Food

Food Testing: It is good to test your food before buying it in the store. You can determine the quality, whether the food has been sprayed with chemicals, or exposed to radiation, whether the food is organic or nonorganic, or if you have an allergic reaction to that particular type of food. There are some factors in a store setting that could affect your results: fluorescent lighting, people, etc., which may mean that it may be best to do some of your more in-depth testing at home. In this way, you can find out what your body really needs and not what you think it wants. It is easy to check for harmony or compatibility of your foods, vitamins, supplements, or anything else that you consume, with the following technique:

- Form your question in your mind and hold it there firmly: for example, "Infinite, is this food for my highest and greatest benefit?" If necessary, continuously repeat the question for each item.

- Adjust your pendulum over the food and allow it to gyrate clockwise or counterclockwise.

- Hold your left hand, palm down, between the pendulum and the food. For most people, the typical response of the pendulum to the back of the hand is a clockwise or positive gyration. If the pendulum continues to gyrate in a clockwise direction after you put your left hand over the food in question, it indicates that there is harmony between you and the food. Should the gyration change direction from positive to negative, or clockwise to counterclockwise, then that food is definitely *not* good for you, (or not good for you at that time). If the pendulum changes to a side-to-side oscillation, this also indicates that the food is not necessarily good or compatible for your needs.

I have witnessed the following in my personal practice and have found this kind of thing to be quite common: a woman with unexplainable headaches went to a doctor who could find no reason for them. The woman used a pendulum held over her food and found a positive response or clockwise direction for brown bread, boiled eggs, etc., and negative response counterclockwise from white bread, fried eggs, sugar, etc. She promptly changed her diet and to this day is free from headaches.

It is also very important to check your household products; your cosmetics and soaps, your cleansers, and anything with deodorants in it. Many of the products we use today contain harmful chemicals that can be the cause of allergies, rashes, headaches, or even low energy.

To test products such as foods, vitamins, herbs, and remedies in relationship to yourself, hold the object or substance in your left hand and suspend the pendulum over it. The motions of the pendulum most often used are: clockwise is positive, compatible, harmonious, or good for you; counterclockwise is negative and not good, incompatible, or inharmonious for you. Again, if your directions are different, that is okay. The important thing is consistency.

When you compare two things that are closely related, you can gauge the difference by the degree or number of the gyrations. For example, you can compare two things, each positive. The greater the degree of movement or the greater the number of gyrations indicates a more positive answer or state.

Another way to determine differences between many potential items of choice is to ask the Intuition to assign a percentage of goodness that a particular product holds for you. This will allow you to test the differences among as many items as you would like, and to choose between items of close likeness. For example, when testing a shelf full of vitamins and minerals, you may come up with levels of "goodness ratings" as, 55%, 65%, 80%, 85%, 90%. You may have one at 98%. This simplifies your comparison and minimizes guesswork. Use of the *Percentage Pendulum Chart* helps to make this process very quick and effective. When you are testing, keep in mind that your *answer is for the immediate time only*. Your results may be different at another time with regard to a particular food, so check often until you have established a consistent record. This is especially important when you test your food for additives or food allergies.

Food additives are sometimes disguised in "codes" and often times are not easily identified. Without knowing just what you are ingesting, subsequent symptoms can be mystifying. If you don't know that "hydrolyzed plant protein" is disguised MSG (monosodium glutamate) you would feel bewildered when you have a reaction. Sometimes food additives can have an impact on one's body that may go completely unnoticed for some time until there is a build up of toxicity from the additive. It is certainly worth your time to check into those food additives your body does *not* benefit from or may even

E104 or E206. There are some books available that give an ordered list of additives and what they do. Using a pendulum while pointing at the additive name, work your way down the list and question, "To what degree does this additive _____ impact my body ___(%),"To what degree does this additive have a less than healthy impact on the well-being of my body ___(%)?", or, "To what degree does this additive have an adverse effect on the well-being of my body?" If there is no list of additives on the product in question, you can check all products for additives that you already know are not beneficial for you. This can be done with any substance that may cause allergic reactions in your system. The questioning for this would be: "Are there any additives in this food _____ that would have less than beneficial impact for my body's well-being?" and, "To what degree ___(%)?" You can apply this process to any substance that you take in, put on your body, or have in your immediate environment.

Sometimes the more common types of allergic reaction to food go unnoticed or are viewed as something to cover up with medication rather than finding the cause for the symptom. For example, a common type of allergic reaction to food is a 'bloated' feeling, burping, or flatulence even after a light meal. The next time you feel heavy or lethargic or have any of the other symptoms mentioned after a meal, write down a complete list of everything you ate. Go through the list using your pendulum and a combination of the *Yes/No Chart* and the *Percentage Chart*. Now precede with questions such as: "Do I have an allergic reaction to ____, to what degree ___(%)?" Note that it may be an allergic reaction to a combination of two or more items or the quantity of

___(%)?" Note that it may be an allergic reaction to a combination of two or more items or the quantity of some of the items being the main cause. Finding the cause of the allergic reaction with combinations of food will take a little more time. It will help to keep a record to see what food combinations come up consistently. With your records you may start to see a pattern with certain combinations. Your next questioning would be: "Do I have an adverse or allergic type reaction to the following combination of _____, _____, _____, _____, to what degree ___(%)?" Try various combinations of foods with the highest percentage being the worst until you feel complete. This will make for a much happier digestive system and inevitably greater well-being.

Quantity & Time

 Figuring Quantity & Time Factor:

Knowing "how much" and " how often" is, by far, the most important factor in taking any kind of medication, vitamin, mineral, homeopathic, etc. Too much too often can be just as bad as none at all and in some cases, even worse.

While you are holding the substance in your left hand, ask: "It is for my highest and greatest benefit to take _____ (for example, Vitamin C, 100 mg., 500 mg., 1000 mg., etc.). Now you will want to figure in the **Time Factor:** "It is best for me to take this once, twice, three, four, times a day, for one, two, three, four days, one week, two, three, one month, two, three," and so forth. It is not necessarily good to take vitamins too often; you could be telling your body to shut down its natural production of a particular vitamin. Sometimes, taking too much of a particular vitamin can be worse than not taking any at all. It is best to find out how much, how often, and this method will help you to establish this information: "It is to my highest and greatest benefit to take this for one, two, three weeks ON, and one, two weeks OFF", etc.... Sometimes, the amount of time *off* is just as important as the amount of time *on*.

To check unknown quantity and time variables with a pendulum: hold the substance while counting the positive (or clockwise) gyrations. You can also use the forward-and-backward (or *Yes*) answer with the pendulum when counting: 1, 2, 3, 4. Perhaps when you get to 5, the swing will start going toward the *Maybe* direction. Then you back off to 4, and you see the swing return to *Yes*. It is good to recheck your answers often and to record the results.

It is a valuable skill to check all your foods, vitamins and supplements (or anything else that you take into your body), and to be able to take the guesswork out of how much, how often. It is always easier to do a preventative maintenance plan than a cure. As the saying goes, "A ounce of prevention is equal to a pound of cure." A little time spent on this practice will be well worth your time. It will prove very beneficial to both the quality of your health and saving of your money. For further work with vitamins, minerals, quantity, and time factors, see the *Pendulum Charts*.

Analysis of the Body

Direct Analysis of the Human Body: Negative conditions or dis-ease in the body can be detected using your Intuition and the pendulum. These negative

of the body part in question, by formulating and asking the appropriate questions, the cause behind the symptoms of the disorder can be determined.

We have the ability to detect any energy distortions or blockages that indicate imbalances within the human body. These imbalances have the potential to become disorders within the body, or may have caused disorders that exist now.

In order to begin, hold the pendulum over the body and begin to form relevant questions. Start with your neutral swing position. Slowly move to different parts of the body and check for the degree of the total health in each area (use ___% for measurement). The pendulum will respond to energy distortions or imbalances by either going to a *No* swing or for most, a counterclockwise gyration. Pain in a particular area of the body may create a negative energy distortion in that area, but the source may be somewhere else. For example, a headache may be caused by a digestion problem. Often, we see that stuffed, blocked, or denied feelings, pain, trauma, or imprints being the cause of the symptoms or physical dis-orders. It is important to define through your questioning what level you are working on; is it physical, mental, emotional, energetic, or etheric. See *Pendulum Charts* for extensive analysis of the human body.

Diagnosing yourself can be one of the trickiest things to do. We want to state categorically that we do not endorse the use of the pendulum as a substitution for seeking help from health care practitioners. It can be difficult to ask questions without an emotional charge or investment in the outcome when health is involved and a charge can prevent accurate answers. We have found that doing our own diagnostic health work can be very helpful in giving our health care practitioners additional information, which in turn can assist them in making a quicker and more accurate diagnosis.

Fertility Cycle: Some women use the pendulum to establish times of highest and lowest fertility for either conception or birth control. This is all right as long as you are not influencing the answers by an unconscious desire to have either a child or sex. If you are going to try this, we would suggest you take a calendar and record your cycle objectively in advance. On the days that you have marked down as the ovulation time, pay close attention to any twinges or other sensations you may feel during ovulation; keep a record and see how accurate you are with your fertility cycle forecasting. This method as a birth control device has an accuracy of greater than 80% for those who have used it. This accuracy rate is comparable to some birth control products currently on the market, and may not be so hard on the body. We suggest that this method be used only if you have had several months of accurate records so that you are sure about your results. Again be aware that your results may be biased due to unconscious desires. This method may be best administered by someone other than the woman in question; this can increase the objectivity of the test and consequently increase the accuracy. Realize also that *anything* can throw off ovulation time. A sudden cold, an emotional shock or charge can trigger or inhibit ovulation. Even if you have an established cycle, use birth control if you want to prevent pregnancy.

Sex Determination: The sex of an unborn child or animal can, at times, be determined by using the pendulum. In some cases, however, we have seen that the unborn baby didn't want their sex to be known before the birthing. The *Yes* swing or for most, the clockwise direction indicating a male, the *No* swing or for most, the counterclockwise indicating a female.

In the case of animals and their multiple births, appropriate questioning will allow you to determine how many males and how many females are in an animal's litter. First, establish how many total animals there are. ("There are 1,2,3.") Then determine the number of males and females. Even the time of birth can accurately be determined by using the techniques described thus far in this book.

This application is currently being used at an egg ranch in Southern California. The pendulum is used over the eggs to determine whether the egg is fertile or not, and whether it contains a male or female chick. The egg production at this ranch has increased immensely. They found that the pendulum user at this ranch can do this type of testing for six hours or more with total accuracy. To try this test yourself, point the egg to the North, suspend the pendulum above the egg and keep your other hand on the table near the egg. A longitudinal swing indicates sterile, clockwise gyration indicates male, and counterclockwise indicates a female.

Animal Analysis

Animal Analysis: You can do analysis on animals in the same manner as previously mentioned for humans. This method can include testing for feeds, medications, supplements, and also for health problems analysis. Use the pendulum to determine the energy blockages and imbalances, or to answer specific questions about a particular symptom or disorder. Animals are less complicated than humans and have no ego involvement to influence the pendulum results. In other words, animals are less apt to produce psychosomatic or placebo responses than humans and easier to get accurate information about more quickly.

Agricultural Analysis

Agricultural: Use the pendulum and this technique to get a better return on your labor. Determine which is the right plant in the appropriate place at the right time, and use the correct fertilizer or soil additives. The objective of this test is to determine whether harmony exists between the plant and the soil, and between the plant and the fertilizer. If a plant is not in harmony with the soil in which it has been planted, it will grow, but it will not thrive. Have you ever wondered why some of the trees or plants we plant do well, and others do not, while some just up and die? Many times we plant trees or crops where WE want them, either for looks or convenience. This may not be what is best for that tree or plant. Have you ever stopped and asked what the tree may want? We do well when we are in a place we want to be, even if the conditions are not perfect. Rarely do we do well in a place we do NOT want to be, regardless of how perfect the conditions may be! So how do we know where the tree wants to be? ASK! That's the gift of the Intuition. We can ask about something we know nothing about and most often get the appropriate answer. For example: "Where on this property is the *best* location to plant this tree that will ensure its health, vigor, and productivity for the longest period of time?" Use the *direction finding, find point method* and/or the *Direction Locator Pendulum Chart*. Once you find a suitable location, you can ask what diameter and depth the hole should be, and which direction the tree should be planted. As a tree grows naturally, it develops a "front door" through which it is believed that energy enters a tree. For the best results, the tree should be replanted with the front door facing in its original direction. You can determine the front door of the tree by using the pendulum technique described in this section.

With the help of the Intuition, you can eliminate the guesswork and have a healthy, happy and abundant plant, garden or crop.

Soil Test: On a piece of paper, place a small sample of the soil from the plot of ground that you are gardening (a large handful is sufficient). About 18" away from the pile of soil, place your plant or seedling. Hold the pendulum over the soil and watch for a strong gyration of the pendulum. Then suspend the pendulum over the plant and watch the gyrations closely. If the pendulum movement indicates a *Yes* or a clockwise direction and increase when the pendulum is placed over the plant, then the plant is in harmony with the soil, and is therefore suitable for growing. If there is a *No* or a counterclockwise direction and decrease, it means that the soil is not particularly good, although not necessarily bad for the purpose. Should the pendulum change to oscillations of forward-and-backward or maybe direction it signifies that the soil requires some form of fertilizer to make it suitable. If the pendulum gyrates the opposite direction when held over the plant, then the soil is unsuitable and no attempt should be made to use it. This test can be applied to anything that grows in the ground, but a living specimen must be used as a sample. If there is an indication that some sort of fertilizer is needed to compensate for some deficiencies, then try the following test.

Soil Nutrient Balance Test: Have samples of about two ounces of each of the fertilizers you may use. Place each substance several inches apart so that they are clear of each other's influence. Hold the pendulum over the plant. When it starts gyrating clockwise or whatever direction you have for Yes, move it above each fertilizer and see which one gives the strongest reaction by the stronger gyrations or the greater number of gyrations. Now, determine how much is required. Slowly add fertilizer in small measured amounts to the heap of soil, and the gyrations will increase. When the maximum is reached the gyrations will decrease. Careful measurement will give exact proportions of fertilizer to soil; too much can also be detrimental. This method can be used for any nutrients that you may wish to use to supplement your plant kingdom.

Automobiles

Automobiles: This procedure has been very successful in diagnosing engine or car problems.

Automobile Exercise 1:

- Hold your pendulum over the engine with the engine off. While your pendulum is gyrating in a *Yes* or clockwise direction, begin to touch the various parts of the engine with your left hand: battery, valves, plugs, carburetor, etc. When a faulty part is touched, the pendulum will come to a stop, change to a *No* or a counterclockwise gyration.

Most answers in this diagnostic will be in the greater-or-lesser degree or percent-of-goodness category. Consequently, we suggest using the counting pendulum language with percentages as to what degree a particular part functions. The direction or movement of the pendulum for measuring greater-or-lesser degrees of will be indicated by varying positions of the *Maybe* direction (between *Yes* and *No*) moving closer to your Yes position as you get closer to 100% correct/true.

There are some dowsers who can tune cars using the pendulum as accurately as those using electronic tune-up equipment. One such dowser, Marcel Trieau, has illustrated this talent many times at the American Society of Dowsers convention. He simply points his finger to various parts of the engine and asks his Intuition to indicate whether that part is in order or not. He can also tell if that particular part is in "so-so" shape by the intensity of the rotations of the pendulum. Trieau is a skilled mechanic and is an example of using a combination of skilled mechanical knowledge and the Intuition to solve complex mechanical problems. He feeds in the proper information from the intellect in order to form the correct questions so that he is able to receive accurate results from his Intuition.

Automobile Trouble-Shooting Exercise 2:

If you have a problem with your car or other mechanical pieces of machinery, get a copy of the schematic of the car, device or equipment. Place it on a table and open to the area of the respective diagram for that part of the system in question. Build in your mind an image of what you feel is wrong with the system; not what you *think* is wrong. Imagine yourself being inside or a part of that system, car or equipment while the problem is taking place. Using a pendulum and a pointer in the other hand, move the pointer around on the schematic asking your Intuition/pendulum to respond when the pointer is over a part of the diagram that represents the cause of the problem. The next step would be to question that part or part's functionality or goodness_____(%).

If you are checking out a car, motorcycle, boat engine, check the basics first such as; "Is it getting gasoline to the carburetor?," "Is the battery charged?," "Is there electrical spark getting to the spark plugs?" These may seem like obvious types of questions, nonetheless, often times the obvious can be overlooked.

Preventive Automobile Maintenance Test 3:

With a diagram of your car in front of you, begin this test by studying it and making a mental image of all the various components of it. Create an image of these various parts and what they mean. Imagine being the car. Ask yourself: "What is the part or system that needs attention?," "What is the functioning level of this part or system___(%)?", "What is the next component that will need replacing?," "Which of the fluid levels need checking or replacing?" Now use your pendulum and a pointer, go over the diagram and/or *Automobile Diagnostics Chart*: let your instrument (pointer on the diagram, pendulum on the *Automobile Diagnostics Chart*) lead you to various points and ask again the questions previously used. Note the results. Do this type of checking on a regular basis. Keep a detailed log book of your results and the comparative analysis of your predictions with the physical reality. Do continue with conventional checking. Learning to know what needs attention before it becomes urgent can save you money and frustration from auto problems on the road.

Generally, your answers will reflect a composite of your skill, experience, and the stored knowledge of your subconscious mind on the subject of the test. However, we have also seen that a person can set out without any prior knowledge regarding the subject and be successful in obtaining accurate results.

Hazard Detection

Noxious Radiations: Test for radiation from underground water, electrical & magnetic appliances and electrical high power lines.

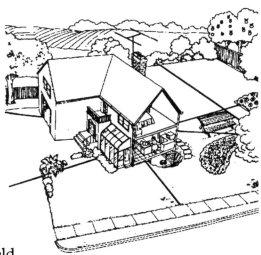

Just because we cannot see a negative energy field

field does *not* mean it cannot hurt us. This is a good example of how our ability to sense the unknown can save us from undue pain and suffering.

It appears that underground water alone, or in combination with some known or unknown ray factor, can be harmful to some plants, animals or people. For example, certain trees will thrive in such areas. Oak, ash, alder, and willow do very well with underground streams. However, if you plant an apple, pear or other fruit tree in such a spot, it may wither and die. Some trees and plants seem to like the underground water and some don't. Animals are the same way. Cats have no objection to sleeping over a stream or so-called irritation zone. Ants make their home over an intersection of two of these streams. Those beehives that house much stronger colonies than others are always over a stream of underground water (The American Dowser, Volume 28, No.2). Yet other animals stay clear of subterranean water. Dogs will sleep out in the open on a wet winter night water rather than in a warm kennel that is over underground water. Pigs prefer to take a newborn litter out into the cold rather than allow them to stay indoors over underground water. Cows seem very sensitive to these irritation zones and seem to produce less milk as a result.

In addition to these factors, there seems to be ample evidence that these elements may be affecting the health of human beings. Even though there is a lack of scientific agreement, the available evidence regarding this correlation between underground streams and adverse effects on the human body is compelling. Research in foreign countries has pointed to a strong correlation between various illnesses and the existence of certain earth energy forces coming from underground running water. Experiments by Dr. Joseph Kopp have suggested that above these subterranean streams and underground water currents several abnormal physical conditions will be found. These include magnetic anomalies, an increase in electrical conductivity of the soil and air, acoustic changes, an increase in the field strength of UHF waves, and an increase in the intensity of infrared radiation. Currently, there is no certainty or understanding of how these underground forces relate to the negative effects that may be produced. Still, enough research has been conducted to suggest that people should avoid places where a dowser gets a negative reaction either from underground water or other suspected underground factors.

Kathe Bachler, in her best selling book, Discoveries of a Dowser, tested 500 cases of people with either malignant or benign tumors and found, without exception, that these people slept over strong earth radiations. Chronic troubles such as arthritis, rheumatism, multiple sclerosis, and asthma are all strong indications of exposure to strong earth radiations. This does not necessarily mean that geopathogenic zones, or their magnetic effects, produce cancer, but it is possible that coupled with an additional antagonist, cancer may be more likely to form under such conditions. Noxious earth radiations can debilitate the human organism by reducing its immunity level.

Pathological effects of sleeping over underground water may take years to become apparent in adults. But in the cases of children, we can see almost immediate effects if they are susceptible to irritation zones. This was demonstrated by Dr. E. Hartman. He put a small baby in a cart which he rolled over an irritation zone. The baby started to cry, but stopped when past the irritation zone. This experiment was repeated several times with the same results.

The energy around the places where we spend a great deal of time can have a profound impact on our health. This is especially true for the sick or disabled who may spend a great deal of time in one place because of their health. (For example, in their beds or chairs.) Since geopathogenic zones can have a deleterious effect, it is especially important that the ill person find a healthy place to live and sleep.

Electro-Magnetic Test: Electromagnetic fields are intangible auras of energy which emanate from all electrical devices, from the biggest power line to the lowliest two-slice toaster. They are composed of two intimately related, but distinct types of energy fields: electric and magnetic. A power line radiates outward to the environment by means of these fields of influence it produces. The following test is for harmful or noxious radiation from: televisions, computer monitors, microwave ovens and other electromagnetic sources.

You will find it interesting to test your television set or microwave oven to see how far noxious radiation from them reaches into your environment. With your pendulum, start as far back as possible and slowly walk toward the object you are testing. Note the location where the movement of the pendulum changes to a negative gyration. Then check from the side of the object. With the television on, I have found the radiation to be as far-reaching as six to ten feet, and with microwave ovens, three to four feet. It is advisable not to let children, animals, or yourself, sit within that negative field. Over time, this noxious radiation can have an adverse effect; it can weaken the immune system and be a factor in causing health disorders.

Experiments in recent years have brought to light many possible links between electromagnetic fields and the increased childhood cancer and leukemia rates.

It now appears that magnetic, rather than electric fields, are most intimately associated with cancer. Normal cellular functioning and development may be disrupted by magnetic pulses.

Small lines carry more current and less voltage than the big lines, making their magnetic fields relatively stronger. While running at only 120 or 240 volts, these lines carry currents higher than the largest power lines. We live in close proximity to these small lines, but are usually quite a distance from high power electrical lines. This is not to say that the high power electrical lines are safe; being in relative proximity to them is very stressful on the human body. We have heard of adverse health problems directly related to living too close to high power electrical lines. High power electrical lines are believed to create direct interference with the central nervous system and can cause neuromuscular confusion, disorientation, and abnormal distribution and absorption of minerals. In our testing of overhead electrical power lines, we have found that adverse effects on the human body can be felt as close as: thirty-five to forty feet for 2,000 volt lines, three-hundred forty to three hundred fifty feet for 230,000 volt lines, etc. You may want to check out the noxious radiation range of overhead power lines in proximity to a house before renting or buying.

Chemical Health Hazards: Using pendulum dowsing as a method to analyze your environment can reveal chemical health hazards or problems which can not be found by conventional medical diagnosis. Micro pollution has been discovered by analytical techniques including gas chromatography, and mass spectrography techniques. Researchers can now analyze contamination in water and food down to parts per billion and parts per trillion. They can detect pesticides, herbicides, toxic industrial chemicals, heavy metals, low level radiation, as well as microwave radiation that can now be detected in our foods and water. All of these harmful substances seem to behave in the same manner on the biological organism. At very low levels they are toxic: they disturb the enzymatic functions, block liver and kidneys, and create serious illness. In general, they create a dis-order called immuno-suppression of the immune system. This disorder can render the immune system weak and ineffective, and it opens us to a host of dis-eases. Examples of such immune system related problems include asthma, allergies, lupus, multiple sclerosis, and arthritis, among others. It is because of such problems with worldwide pollutants showing up in our food and water that I feel so compelled to teach people how to determine what is and what is not for their highest and greatest benefit. As with most of the previous applications, the counting-percentage method for measuring the degree of goodness can be quite effective. See *Pendulum Charts.*

Business

Business Decisions: On the job and in business, using the Intuition can give you a great advantage over the normal trial-and-error

approach to decision-making. If you are wavering between two alternatives in a business situation, you can use your Intuition, pendulum, *Yes/No* language and/or *Percentage Charts* to find the best course of action. Using the Intuition is an excellent way to help give you a boost in making up your mind regarding appropriate choices. Additional applications might be the use of the Intuition in locating a specific area or item such as a building site for a business, the perfect store front, the right tool or truck, etc. A very effective use of the Intuition in business is to determine the best employee for a particular job. Finding the best employee to hire can be very tedious, time consuming, and, the best employee may not always be apparent from the application. This task can be greatly facilitated by taking your stack of applications and resumes, reading the name of the applicant and scanning pages of the application. Put your left (receiving) hand over the signature or photo, use your pendulum and *Percentage Chart*, determine to what degree this applicant would be best suited in filling the open position, assign a percentage to this individual, and then move on to the next applicant. I have found this to be very effective and accurate, especially when there are many closely qualified candidates and the determining factor cannot be gauged from the application.

The Intuition can also be used in sales to locate prospects and prospective areas, or in land deals where it may be necessary to locate water or minerals. One of the most effective uses of the pendulum might be in telephone conversations where a snap decision needs to be made, or to determine the validity or truth of what is being said.

Using your Intuition in weighing the pros and cons of any situation before making a business decision can save you a great deal of time, effort, and money. The more you use and develop your Intuition, the more you will find ways to use it in business and/or personal life applications. This can result in greater quality and success in your life.

Years ago, I had a construction company and needed to make contracting bids on a regular basis. For many in the business, this is a procedure that could take one day to one or more weeks of detailed planning, telephoning, and footwork to determine the total figure to submit to the customer. In most cases, if the contractor does not get the job, most, if not all, of the time required to make the bid is uncompensated. After having been in the trade for quite a few years, I did have a fairly good idea as to the cost of things; nonetheless, I didn't like all the time it took for figuring bids and estimates. I started to use my Intuition and pendulum to determine the right cost figure of the job for both myself and the customer. After checking out the job site and talking with the potential customer, I would go out to my van and come up with the appropriate estimate by using my Intuition. At first, to determine the right figure, I would ask myself: "How badly do I need this job?" "How tough is the competition?"

or "Can the customer afford what their ideas will cost?" However, I found that this type of questioning could be somewhat fear-laden, and that could have a negative effect on the results of the test.

More inclusive types of statements that I found to give the best results were: "It would be to my highest and greatest benefit to take on this job with _____ (customer name)" If *Yes*, then, "Infinite, indicate the perfect cost figure of this job for _____ (customer) that will be for the highest and greatest benefit of _____ (customer) and myself?" This procedure would take me all of five minutes, and to my customer's surprise I would come back with the bid or estimate in hand. The surprised looks on the faces of my customers were always fun, for typically my figures were directly aligned with theirs. Comments like, "Well, that's exactly what I had in mind- when can you start?" were quite normal. The interesting thing about this was, I always got the job and I always had great customers.

Sometimes the jobs ended up taking more time or more money, but, usually the customers were great about it and balanced out the overrun cost. As the result of using my Intuition, I know without a doubt that overall I made better decisions in a fraction of the time and saved both my customers and myself a great deal of time and money with a minimum amount of stress. The Intuition was also incredibly helpful in on-the-job trouble-shooting, usually leaving the customers and the other tradespeople amazed as to how I was able to solve problems so quickly, even with many unknown factors.

Treasure

Finding Treasure: Almost all treasure hunters seem to have one main problem in common. They can do the research— rummage through dusty old records, newspapers, and stale-smelling court records, find out who did what to, and with whom, and work out accurately the best location where the treasure is most likely to be found. However, when they finally arrive on the scene, most often, they still cannot dowse exactly the

 right spot; they cannot just march up to one spot and say, "Dig here!" and after digging, find the treasure! They can find the general location without difficulty, but NOT the exact location! We have seen this to be true on numerous occasions. There are many reasons for such apparent failure. There may be powerful "thought-forms" surrounding the buried treasure. Influential energy of those who hid the treasure may, in a sense, still be guarding it. There seem to be many things and events that can confuse the area of the search, making it next to impossible to find the exact spot or *find point*. I have heard myself saying quite often, "Oh well, if it wereeasy, somebody would have already found it." Before you go out and attempt dowsing the location of some hidden treasure, you should first teach yourself to find hidden objects. Once this is accomplished, have someone "dirty-up" the location with artificial *thought-forms*, and try again. Anyone who can learn to do this on a consistent basis will greatly enhance his chances for finding the real thing.

With practice and common sense, you will learn what the pendulum (Intuition) will and will not answer for you. Much will depend on where the limitations are in your thinking or belief systems at any particular time or place. Your only limitations are the ones you believe in.

There are always solutions to every situation or challenge. If you should find yourself in a position of an immovable impasse, get others to assist you with your search for truthful answers. If you need assistance, the author is available for consultations.

Chapter 7

Pendulum Charts

The *Pendulum Charts* are very effective in keeping the intellect or ego entranced long enough to allow the Intuition to function with little interference from the so-called rational mind. Additionally, the charts allow the Intuition to communicate about the subject through questions that you may not have thought of asking. The charts will give you numerous ideas about different things to look for and different ways to ask pertinent questions. *Sometimes you can learn more from the questions than you can from the answers.* These pendulum charts are "user friendly;" the more you work with them, the more you will discover ways to use them and the more you will learn how to adapt them to many other types of applications. Use the *Knowing Your Intuitive Mind Pendulum Chart Applications* as the software interface between the Intuition and the conscious mind.

Working with the pendulum charts can be very helpful in learning how to phrase and flow questions, however, it is not possible to have all the questions ready made for you. It does take a fair amount of practice to determine the questions that will clearly and precisely state the depths of your questions. This is why it is so important to start out simply, then practice and practice. We suggest keeping it simple by first starting with finding the correct foods or vitamins, etc. for your body and practice and practice before you get into doing questions around life complexities and challenges.

When you work with these charts, remember to do the *threefold permission* before you start, especially if it involves others. It is imperative that you have permission and that you determine the appropriateness of your line of questioning.

You will discover that the applications are infinite for finding answers about yourself or others. The *witness* method described herein has proven to be a quick and accurate means to access intuitive information and knowledge.

Each chart is described, and you will read about lines of questioning to consider as you attempt to uncover information. Remember, this is a dynamic and interactive process that will require your focused attention and creativity. As always, your answers will be only as good as your questions.

Master Chart

Master Chart: This is the menu for starting. This chart will assist you in beginning your line of questioning for a particular situation, dilemma, or challenge. This is the lead-in to all other charts when you have no clues as to a starting point. When you get to the end of a line of questioning, or come to a blank state of mind, it is good to refer back to this *Master Chart* and ask if there are any other charts that would be helpful in approaching the particular situation in question. Remember to keep in mind all variables, including your state of mind, energy level, and the proper time and place.

Pendulum Language Chart

Pendulum Language: If you haven't already established your communication line with your Intuition, this is the beginning point for you. Read the section on establishing the pendulum language (Chapter 2), and the basic instruction enclosed with the pendulum charts. Review Yes/No, forward-and-backward, side-to-side, clockwise and counterclockwise language. *Maybe* is more-or-less degrees of swing between the *Yes* and *No* positions. If you get no motion, or erratic motion, try again at another time or rephrase the question. If your pendulum language is different than what has been presented here as the most commonly used directions, remember that you are the one in charge and the Intuition wants to establish a language that will work best for you. It may require making some adjustments with your pendulum language in order to effectively work with the pendulum chart systems. Find what works best for you.

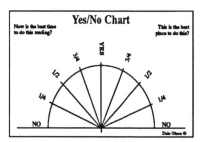

Yes/No Chart

Yes/No Chart: This is the most commonly used chart in combination with other charts. Before starting your line of questioning it is best to get in the habit of asking declarative statements to measure the variables that can affect your accuracy: "Now is the best time to do this reading or questioning?" and

"This is the best place to do this questioning" and the *threefold permission* (may I, can I, should I). This is a great chart to determine answers that are not only *Yes* or *No*, but also a *Maybe* answer or degrees of *Yes/No*. The answers to most questions will fall into the category of *Maybe* or more-or-less. Most often you will be using this chart in conjunction with other charts and the **Percentage-Probability Chart.**

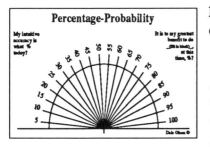

Percentage-Probability Chart

Percentage-Probability: Along with your **Yes/No Chart**, this will be the most widely used chart for comparing two or more like products, variables or choices. You may find that ascribing percentages to various factors will be most helpful in determining differences that may seem otherwise ambiguous. In other words, you can compare multiple variables and assign percentages to each, thereby putting your choices on a scale of most beneficial to least beneficial. In this way, problems can be weighed and choices made much easier. The main factor to keep in mind is how you word your questions to the Intuition. Be clear and precise, measure one variable at a time, and remember the time factor; what was true yesterday may not be so today. After using the **Yes/No Chart** to determine if time and place is appropriate for the test, it is then beneficial to use the **Percentage-Probability Chart** to ask, "My intuitive accuracy is what ____% today?" Then you may proceed with your questioning. "Is it for my highest and greatest benefit to do or check out

_____ at this time, to what percent ___%?" This chart can be used in conjunction with all other charts to measure or weigh any variable or combination of factors or choices. This chart is also very useful in determining the probability of success for a particular situation, event, or experience.

Alphabet-Numerical Chart

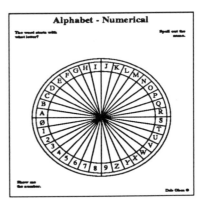

Alphabet-Numerical: This chart is to assist in spelling out a name, word, or number unknown to the conscious mind. This can be helpful in spelling out the names of your guides, teachers, or the names of places and things within your subconscious or collective consciousness. This chart can also be used in determining a sequence of numbers. Please keep in mind not to treat this like a Ouija board, which can involve boundary issues but also may invite unwanted energies or influences resulting in misinformation, confusion and potentially a decrease in your well being.

There can be a temptation to inquire about subjects that may stem from one's curiosity or ego. This line of questioning could result in decreasing one's skill to that of a parlor game. Your best gauge for safety and accuracy is to discern beforehand from within your most sacred, balanced and grounded place as to what information is appropriate and to everyone's highest and greatest benefit.

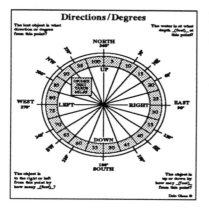

Directions-Degrees-Depth Chart

Directions-Degrees-Depth: This is a three-dimensional chart. You can use this chart for finding a lost person, pet, object, buried treasure, archaeological site, water, oil, or minerals (such as crystals, gold, silver, etc.). What you are looking for can be miles away or hundreds of feet beneath the surface of the ground. It is still within our intuitive abilities to find them. This may be difficult to comprehend, and it may not be acceptable to the logical part of the brain. Nonetheless, it has been clearly evidenced throughout history that people have found water, gold, lost people, and many other things by using their Intuitive abilities.

A substantiated example of this ability is with the oil companies. Most of the leading oil companies in the world employ people to do what is referred to as "map dowsing" with a pendulum. Some of the major oil finds in the world today have been discovered through this method. (For further details on map dowsing, see chapter eight on "distance dowsing".)

All people, all substances on this planet, radiate at a certain energetic frequency or set of frequencies. Dowsing is a means of tuning into that frequency within a certain area. By using your intention and focusing your mind, you tune into the parameters of the frequency of that particular person, lost object, or buried treasure.

Use this chart in conjunction with a map. Orient your map and this chart to magnetic North (use a compass). Begin by placing a dot on the map at a location within the *search* area. Place the dot on the map at a familiar landmark (post, surveyor's marker, river, rock formation, etc.). Now you can use your chart: "Infinite, the lost object is what direction or what degree from this point?," or, "The object is to the right or left from this point by how many _____inches, feet, yards, miles ?" or "The water is at what depth _____feet at this point ?" or "The object is up or down by how many _____feet from this point?" and so forth.

It will take some practice to develop the ability to locate lost or buried objects or substances. We suggest that you start with things that you can find the answer to (such as known buried water or electric lines) or practice by having someone bury an object (like a ring or something to which you are attached.) Then go and locate it. Start simply and build slowly to develop this skill; starting too big can be very discouraging. Remember that this is a learning process, so build on your skills and practice.

An example of using the direction-degrees chart and long distance dowsing was in finding a missing dog and the dognapper. This is one of my happiest success stories in which a dog had been stolen by someone's ex-partner and taken to the other side of the country. The owner knew that the dog was somewhere in California. We acquired a state map, and city maps of Los Angeles and San Francisco. On my advise, the owner went to San Francisco where I felt the dog to be located and was working along with the police and the court system. We were getting varying locations at different times and were able to pinpoint the exact locations by first getting the appropriate direction (N-S-E-W) from the center of the map and refining it down to exact streets and the house in which the dog was being held. The dog was being moved from house to house to avoid the police. Finally, after two weeks of a cat-and-mouse game with the dognapper, the dog, police and the court system (to provide the proper legal papers), we were able to pinpoint and coordinate the exact place and time for all the players in this game to be present. This was a success story and the owner and the dog were happily reunited.

This was a success story and I love relating it, but unfortunately some are painfully not. From this story I hope you can see that locating an animal or missing person can take a great deal of patience, persistence, perseverance and determination. In the above story there were times when I could easily have thought that the intuitive answers to be erroneous and could have started to question my own abilities. This is when *trust must prevail.*

There is one note of caution on searching for lost people or animals. The people or animals you are looking for may not consider themselves lost, and/or they may not want to be found. This could have a major effect on the accuracy of your results.

Personal Motivators Chart

Personal Motivators: This chart helps you to run checks and balances on your emotions. This can determine both positive and negative aspects and can pinpoint emotional imbalance. By using the percentage chart in conjunction with this chart, you can determine to what degree a particular personal motivator prevails in your life at the present time. If there is some question as to why you want to do a particular thing or what is behind making a particular choice: "The present issue evolves around which personal motivator _____, and to what percent ___(%)?" This will indicate very quickly whether your decision is based on a true positive emotion or out of fear or ego.

Relationship Compatibility Chart

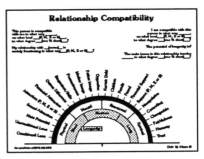

Relationship Compatibility: This chart, in conjunction with the percentage chart, can be used to determine what level of compatibility exists with the people in your life. You can use this chart in a myriad of ways to measure or compare the aspects and attributes of a relationship between you and another person (your mate, children, family, friend, partner, employer, employee, teacher, physician, therapist, and so forth).

With the *Relationship Compatibility Chart,* begin your line of questioning with, "This person is compatible with me in what way _____ ?," and visa versa, "Indicate what other variables are involved in this relationship with _____ ?" and "To what degree is this variable part of the relationship ____%."

Although doing this type of inquiry can assist you in being clear about your own desires or ulterior motives toward the person in question, it can be tricky to keep your objectivity when checking out others in relationship to yourself. It is rare that one can ask about relationship compatibility from a completely neutral space. Most often the truth can prevail with very interesting results. The answers can indicate information quite different than what you may have thought was true. This difference of answers and prior thought sometimes is indicative of objective truthful answers due to the fact that what we want to hear often times prevails. As with all areas of questioning where our neutrality is questionable we suggest using other methods of verification, for example, the three card method or getting another person to also check it out for you.

We have seen this chart used for checking the potential longevity of a relationship. Remember, any time you start questioning about the future, you stand the chance of being incorrect. Time factors are the hardest to predict because you or the person involved can change your mind(s) at any moment, thereby changing the end results. Another drawback to figuring longevity of relationships is that the future plans may not yet be established in the other person's mind.

In other words, keep the questioning light and easy, and do not take it too seriously, especially at the outset. If you are getting some negative results about the individual in question day after day, and you really feel that the results are from the truth of your inner knowingness, respond in a manner that is true to your self and to your highest benefit. It is also very beneficial to complete your line of questioning by asking, "Am I in this relationship because there are some very valuable lessons for me to learn about my _____(self, life, strength, personal power, character, others, etc.)?"

We interact with other people on four levels: physical, mental, emotional, and spiritual. Consequently, compatibility is more complex than it may seem because we must compare compatibility on each of these four levels. Questioning in this area has depth beyond our normal linear perspective. This is important because you cannot look at the whole issue of compatibility without considering each of these four levels. Your questions must be specific in regard to these distinctly different, yet sometimes overlapping levels of existence.

Within your line of questioning, it is best to consider your compatibility to the other person, and also the other person's compatibility to you on each of these levels. This is where you can work with the *Percentage Chart* to weigh the various aspects and attributes within the relationship. For example, the line of questioning would be, "I am compatible with this person in what way _____ (aspect or attribute) on what level _____(physical, mental, emotional, spiritual) to what degree ____ %" (use *Percentage Chart*)" and _____(name) is compatible with me in what way _____ (attribute/aspect) on what level _____ (physical, mental, emotional, spiritual) to what degree ____ %." By following this line of questioning, you may become aware of which aspects and attributes contributed to your attraction to the other person. You may also understand the differences in compatibility on each of the four levels, and how you both focused on each other.

115

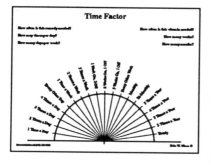

Time Factor Chart

Time Factor: The Time Chart needs to be used in conjunction with other charts to determine the appropriate time factor involved with the use of vitamins, minerals, remedies, therapy treatments, exercise programs, food supplements, the need for particular foods, herbs, fertilizers, etc. For example, "This vitamin is needed how often ?" Determine whether it is to be taken on a continuous basis or how many weeks "*on*" and how many weeks "*off*." Sometimes a program with a certain number of weeks *on* and a number of weeks *off* may prove to be the most beneficial. Too much of a good thing can sometimes be worse than nothing at all. Be sure you determine the correct time factor of what you are measuring so that it can be used for your highest and greatest benefit.

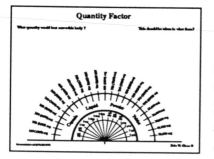

Quantity Factor

Quantity Factor: This is similar to the time factor chart because it can be used in conjunction with anything that has volume or mass to it-anything that requires an unknown measurement that is most appropriate for the individual or application. This chart can be useful for determining the quantity of vitamins, minerals, supplements, herbs, remedies, fertilizer, etc. The line of questioning would be, "The most appropriate

need for this _____ is in what quantity _____ and
how often _____?"

Plant-Soil Chart

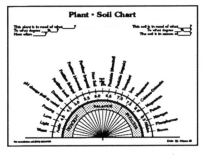

Plant-Soil: As mentioned
earlier, you can make a
plant grow under some
pretty adverse conditions,
but you cannot make it
thrive. Most people expect
that all a plant needs is to be planted and then expect it
to go well. When the plant hardly comes to blossom, or
produces very little fruit, they are greatly disappointed.
This is the unfortunate result of the trial-and-error
approach. By tuning into the plant, and by your intention
directing your communication to the life force within the
plant, you will have great success in determining exactly
what the plant needs for optimum production. The *Plant-
Soil Chart* can show you exactly what is needed in soil
conditions (pH scale), fertilizer, water, light, etc. Try the
pH scale to determine whether the soil is acidic or alkaline
by holding your left hand over a sample of soil while
using your pendulum with the pH scale. If you have a
chemical pH tester, run another physical pH test and
compare the two. You may find that the two pH tests
will be the same or very close. You can also at any time
determine whether the plant or soil is deficient, balanced,
or has an excess of something.

Condition Chart

Condition: This chart can be used at the start of a test
to determine the degree to which a particular problem

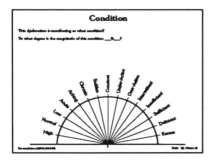

exists, the condition of a particular organ or area of the body, or the overall state of health of the individual being tested. The chart is designed to handle many different physical, mental, or emotional conditions. For example, you can determine the condition of blood pressure or temperature, degree of dysfunction, disease, or disorder, or the activity level of glands or organs. The line of questioning would be something like, "This _____ (individual, dysfunction, disorder, disease, organ, gland, etc.) is exhibiting what condition _____ and to what degree ____%?"

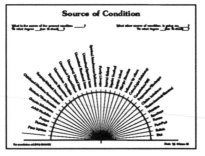

Source of Condition Chart

Source of Condition: This chart covers the source or causation behind most of the existing symptoms that an individual can manifest. This is not to be interpreted as the final word about a particular dis-order or dis-ease; however, it does help to find the doorway through which one may approach the remedy that will be most effective. You may find there are more sources of conditions than could be added to the *Source of Condition Chart*. You may also have other sources of conditions based on different belief systems. These you will uncover yourself.

The line of questioning would be: "The present condition of_____ (type of condition) with _____(name of individual) is from what source _____, and to what degree___(%)?"

Origin of the Dis-ease Chart

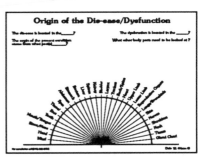

Origin of the Dis-ease: This chart indicates in which part of the body the present condition or symptom began. You can also use it for finding the body part where the present condition exists, or where there may be a potential for problems to arise. In many cases, the results may point to an area where the individual has stuffed emotions and/or imprints from past traumatic experiences. You may also find physical trauma or energetic imprint residue left in the body from accidents many years ago. This type of imprinting from a trauma may not always be seen on the physical level as problematic symptoms; however, we have seen hundreds of cases where such energetic imprints, in time, turned into dis-order or dis-ease. The line of questioning would be: "The (disease, disorder, symptom, origin, potential problem) is located where in the body _____, and it is (physical, mental, emotional, energetic) _____ (Yes/No), and to what degree___(%)?"

Healing Remedies

Healing Remedies: The Healing Remedy Chart covers methods from conventional to alternative forms of

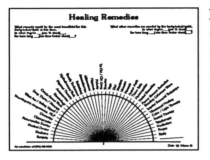

healing. You may find that there are some forms of healing that are not listed and can be added. It is best to make this chart span the range of healing forms within your own belief system. Even if you are not completely familiar with some of the listed modes of healing, stay open; they may be totally effective and useful for you or someone else. We have found that usually more than one type of healing modality may be required. The line of questioning would start with: "For total health and well-being of; ____(individual's name)____, for the ___(symptom, dysfunction, disorder, disease)___, he/she is in need of what remedy _____, to what degree ____(%)?" and "This body is in need of what other remedy _____ to what degree ____(%)?"

Weighing the choices by using percentages gives you a way to compare two or more types of healing modalities. This will enable you to make intuitive choices that will assist you in deciding which is the most effective, safe, and least traumatic approach. It will also help to determine the appropriate order of the therapies. Adding the time factor to the acquired information will give an additional dimension, finding both the most effective means for the healing process and when it would be best to start or end one particular type of therapy. This "fine tuning" will help you to determine the most effective form of therapy at the right time resulting in the least amount of trauma, with greater healing results in a shorter time period, and usually with less financial cost.

Systems of the Body Chart

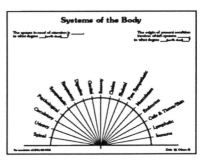

Systems of the Body: This chart helps to give an overview to determine what systems are involved with the dysfunction or dis-ease. The line of questioning is: "The system in need of attention is _____, to what degree ____(%)?" Sometimes what may appear to be a symptom originating from one part of the body may in fact have its origin in another area of the body or system. This chart can be most beneficial in determining potential dysfunction or dis-orders. Being able to weigh each system using percentages can be a great asset in a preventative maintenance program for yourself or others.

Glandular (Endocrine) System Chart

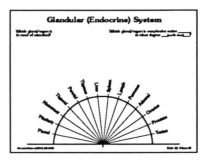

Glandular System: This chart is based on the glands of the endocrine system which control most body functions through chemicals called hormones. The activity of these glands can have a drastic influence on the health or balance of the body, as well as the mental or emotional balance of the mind. The line of questioning would be: "Infinite, indicate which of these glands are functioning improperly, _____, and to what degree ____(%)?" or for an overall type of testing, "To what degree is the gland _____ (go through all glands one at a time) functioning properly _____(%)?"

Chakra System Chart

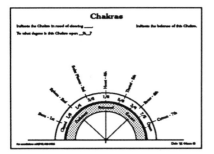

Chakra System: The chakras are energy centers that are connected within and throughout the energy system of the body. These energy centers were identified in ancient times, and we now have the technological equipment to measure these centers and verify their existence. Some people are able to "see" these energetic centers of the body.

With this chart you can determine how open or closed a particular chakra is. This indicates how well the energy is flowing to a particular area or how much blockage there is in that area. This will also determine the vitality or total health of the organs within that area. You can determine which chakras are not functioning properly by having the Intuition indicate to what degree these centers are open, whether the energy is deficient, balanced, or in excess.

The line of questioning with this chart would be: "Infinite, indicate the Chakra associated with present symptoms, disorders, issues _____?" or "Indicate how open this chakra is_____." "Indicate the degree of balance of this particular chakra _____." We have found it to be very beneficial to measure someone's chakras before using a form of therapy and then measuring them afterwards to determine the effectiveness of that particular therapy. The benefit or effectiveness of the therapy will show up immediately within the chakras. This is a great form of feedback that can be quite beneficial for the client.

To see an improvement when measuring the chakras assists in the integration of that improvement into his/her belief system.

There is a great deal more that can be learned about the chakra system. We have seen it to be an incredibly accurate and dynamic way of determining the total health of the physical, mental, emotional, and etheric states of being. In years to come, we feel that an analysis of the chakra system will become the main form of diagnosis of the human body. For an extensive and accurate view on the chakra system, we would suggest reading <u>Wheels of Life</u> by Anodea Judith.

Remember that these charts are not a substitute for medical care and should not be seen as such. Please consult your physician or other health care provider.

Color Radiation & Color Need Chart

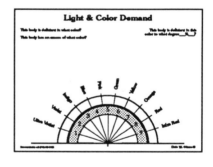

Color Radiation & Color Need: This chart corresponds with the *Chakra System Chart* and is another way of indicating to what degree the body or chakra is deficient in a particular energy/color. In this case, light and color radiating at certain frequencies is considered to be a necessity and is utilized by the body in order to remain vital, balanced, and healthy. The origin of this perspective comes from ancient times; metaphysics and today's science are now beginning to accept that color and light play a vital part in the health and wellness of the human being. The line of questioning for this chart would be: "Infinite, this body _____ is deficient in what color _____ and to what degree _____ (1-9 scale or %)? and "This body _____ is in excess of what color _____, to what degree ____(1-9 scale or %)?"

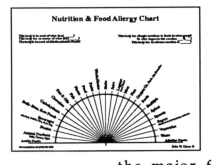

Nutrition & Food Allergies Chart

Nutrition & Food Allergies: This chart is used to determine where there may be a deficiency or excess in one or more of the major food groups. The most widespread use of this chart is to find what food allergies exist in what major food groups. Once that is determined, you can make your own list of all the food types within that major group consumed by the individual being tested. From there you can find the foods that are responsible for allergic reactions. This can be accomplished with either a *Yes/No* or a percentage answer to your list of potential allergenic foods. The line of questioning would be: "Infinite, the body of _____(name) is in need of what food(s) _____(food group, specific types), to what degree ____(%)?" "This body _____(name) is in excess of what food(s) _____(food group, specific types), to what degree ____(%)?" or "This body _____(name) has allergic reactions to what food(s) _____(food group, specific types), and to what degree _____(%)?"

Food Supplement Chart

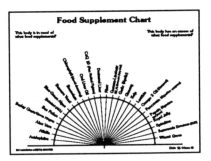

Food Supplements: This chart can be helpful to those who may be in need of supplements to their ordinary diet. Sometimes these may be appropriate for chronic conditions or for those who find today's foods lacking in the necessary nutrition for total health and well-being. There are more food supplements that could be added to this list and for some of you, there are some that could be eliminated. Again, we suggest that you change this chart to correspond to whatever works for you. The line of questioning for this chart would be: "Infinite, this body _____ (name) is in need of what nutritional supplement _____, to what degree _____ (%)?"

Vitamin Chart

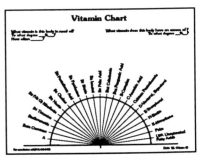

Vitamin Chart: Choosing the correct vitamins, for your own needs or for others, can be accomplished with this chart. Most people choose their vitamins by guessing or because someone told them the supplement would be good for them, or because they read something about a particular vitamin and therefore feel they need it. Sometimes they may even be correct when they think they need a certain vitamin. Often the body will "yell loudly," so to speak, to let us know we have a need. Sometimes we actually even hear it.

It is a well-established fact that the vitamin and mineral content of our foods is much diminished from what it was many years ago. Consequently, we find ourselves needing to supplement our diets to fulfill the requirements of our demanding lifestyles. Using this chart to fine-tune your need for a particular vitamin can be of great value to you. Using the typical "shotgun method" of vitamin-taking can be detrimental, too much of a good thing can be just as harmful as not taking anything at all. Selecting the correct vitamins at the right time, and taking them for the appropriate duration can make a world of difference in the results you get. The line of questioning would be; "Infinite, the vitamins that would be the most beneficial for _____(name)_____ are _____(vitamins list)_____, to what degree ____(%), and how often _____(Time Factor Chart)?"

If you have a group of vitamins and minerals that you already use daily, line the bottles up in front of you. Point to each one and ask,"Does my body need the contents (Vitamins/Minerals) of this bottle today?", "To what degree ____(%)?" If Yes, than use Quantity & Time Factor Charts and determine how much how often. Sometimes less is more. Also keep in mind that quantity can vary from day to day. This can sound like a lot of work, however, with practice the time to do this can be dramatically reduced, taking only a few minutes to do the entire job. Record your results over a period of time. You may find patterns. Do you notice any difference in general health or energy level as you vary your additive intake or quantity? Have you saved money by taking only the additives that your body is in need of? Doing this type of qualitative and quantitative fine tuning can be applied to all that you take in.

Minerals & Elements Chart

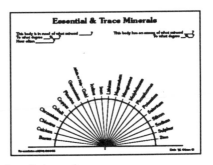

Minerals & Elements: This chart is similar to the *Vitamin Chart* except that it has additional elements. Because of some of today's agricultural practices, our food is often stripped of much of its nutritive value. It is getting harder to acquire the necessary amount of vitamins, minerals, and trace elements from our foods for our bodies to assimilate for vitality and overall health. This is why we need to check on a regular basis to see whether we are getting enough from our foods and whether we need to supplement our diet with vitamins, minerals, and trace elements. This chart also contains some elements which allow you to check for excesses; as mentioned previously, excess can be as unhealthy as a deficiency. The line of questioning would be: "Infinite, this body is in need of what mineral _____, to what degree ___(%)?" or "This body is in excess of what mineral _____, and to what degree ___(%)?"

Tissue Salts Chart

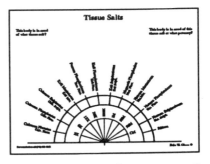

Tissue Salts: The Tissue Salts (cell salts) are the trace elements (on the cellular level) that are essential to the life and well-being of the human organism. Much research has shown that dis-ease and pain will result from an imbalance or deficiency of the tissue salts in the human body. This chart will help you to choose the needed tissue salt(s), and also aid in determining the potency level of the tissue salts needed for relief and/or balanced health. It is equally important to determine the appropriate timing (see Time Factor Chart) in this analysis for effective tissue salt use. The line of questioning would be: "Infinite, this body is in need of what tissue salt _____, to what degree ___(%), at what potency _____(3X, 6X, 12X, 30X, or higher dosages), for how long _____(1 week, 2 weeks, 1 month,...)?" Before going out and buying tissue salts we would suggest that you consult a naturopathic doctor, and read The 12 Tissue Salts by Esther Chapman.

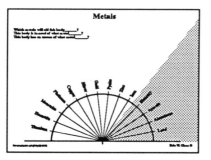

Metals Chart

Metals: This chart can help to determine which of the metals would be beneficial to have on or around the body, and which of the metals may be creating a high level of metal toxicity within the body. This chart can also be used for prospecting for precious minerals. The line of questioning would be: "Infinite, which of the metals would be for the greatest benefit of this body _____(name), and to what degree ____(%)?" and "This body has a metal toxicity of what metal _____, and to what degree ____(%)?" For prospecting, the line of questioning would be: "Infinite, indicate which metals are present in this rock sample _____, and to what level of concentration _____(1/8, 1/6, 1/4, 1/2, 1, 2, ... ounces per ton)?"

Gemstones & Quartz
Gemstones Chart

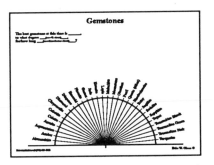

Gemstones & Quartz
Gemstones: The use of this
chart is a necessity for those
who are wearing or using
crystals and gemstones for
therapeutic purposes. A great deal of the printed material
on the subject of gemstones is vastly lacking in accuracy
and validity. We suggest that you find out what is true
for you when it comes to choosing crystals and gemstones
for certain healing aspects and attributes. Each stone
has a particular energy vibration which can affect the
human body. Inappropriate stones at the wrong time
can have a debilitating effect on the human body due to
an overcharging of the nervous system. Because of all
the misinformation circulating about the mineral
kingdom, it is imperative that we learn how to use our
Intuition to choose the appropriate crystals and
gemstones. We need to know the appropriate gemstone
for a particular need.

It is equally important to find out the best place to wear
a gemstone and how long it should be worn The line of
questioning would be: "Infinite, the best gemstone for
this situation or application is _____, to what
degree ____(%)?" "The best gemstone for this dis-order,
dysfunction, etc... is _____, and to what degree
____(%), placed on the body or worn for how long
_____(10, 20, ...minutes, or up to 1, 2, ...days, weeks,
months), and the best place to wear this gemstone is
_____ (pendant crystal termination up/down,
fingers, wrist, solar plexus, pocket, etc.)?"

Blank Charts

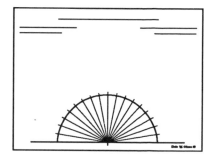

Blank: There are blank charts so that you can make up your own charts which can accommodate your particular belief systems, desires, or forms of therapy. You will find that you can create charts on any subject to assist you in answering most questions. Regardless of your area of questioning (personal, business, interest, or hobby), there are no limits to your questioning except your own self-imposed limits on your beliefs.

The charts and the questions you ask will assist you in developing communication with your Intuition in a relatively short period of time. After you have worked with these charts for a while, you will find your left brain becoming very involved with the line of questioning as well as with the visual focus on the charts. After a few moments, you will find yourself slipping into a slightly altered state of consciousness in which your perception will feel defocused, while the questioning seems to continue with crystal clarity at a fast rate. At this point you may find some of the questions and answers to be different from what you may normally think about the situation at hand.

In doing a complete analysis of the physical, mental, emotional, and spiritual aspects of an individual (sometimes taking as long as one and one-half hours), I have found myself in what feels like a time warp. There is no longer an awareness of time. When I finish the process, I am always surprised at how much time has passed. Typically the session leaves me feeling very energized, meditative, with a clear sense of having seen the truth behind the questioning. Most often the answers vary immensely from what I may have thought was true at the the start of the questioning. There is usually the feeling of having seen the bigger picture and how it all fits perfectly together for that person or situation, regardless of how it may appear. The choices that you, or the individual being tested have made about certain life experiences become apparent. Then I can see all of the options clearly and help the person to accurately choose the one option that will be for their highest and greatest benefit, which is in alignment with their life's purpose, desires, or goals.

Chapter 8

Distant & Map Dowsing

The Intuition is not limited to the physical plane and therefore is not restricted to Time and Space (Distance).

"Map dowsing" is a term used to define the use of the Intuition to locate persons, animals, objects and substances either above, in, or below ground or water. The work is done from a distance, by means of a pointer, map, chart, photo, or dowsing instrument.

As discussed earlier, the scientific approach with use of a pendulum is called *radiesthesia,* which means detecting, measuring, or locating the entire spectrum of radiation (energy) that is coming from something. This may be an object, substance, mineral, plant, animal, or human. If you are dowsing from a long distance away it is called *distant dowsing or teleradiesthesia.* Map and distance dowsing are forms of intuitive communication utilizing charts, diagrams, photos, documents, letters, signatures, or samples from the area of the quest. The application of distant dowsing can include searching for minerals, metals, precious stones, mines, tunnels, buried treasure, old monuments, foundations, graves, archaeological sites, artifacts, ships, schools of fish, lost aircraft, vehicles, missing people, bodies, pets, oil, water, money, valuables, and many other things. Map and distance dowsing are almost one and the same; the main difference is that one procedure uses a map, and the other uses a photo of a person, or a *witness* (sample). The "witness" consists of an object owned or worn by the person or a sample of the substance involved in the search. It is believed that the witness aids the dowser in focusing and concentrating on (or perhaps creating an affinity with) the person, object, or substance of the search.

The object, substance, or area of the search may be hundreds or thousands of miles away, or buried many feet below the surface. Some people may have a problem accepting this form of intuitive fact-finding. The thought of being able to pass a pendulum over a map and locate an object or person seems a little farfetched to many people. However, when you first started to develop your intuitive abilities, the thought of being able to use the Intuition to *search* for some of the previous types of unknowns may have seemed almost impossible. Map and distant dowsing may seem inconceivable to some, but so do many other phases of the art of dowsing.

Thought Forms

Where the thought goes, the energy flows.

Thoughts can travel great distances with no time frame involved, as indicated by Marcel Vogel's experiments with plants. Marcel presented clear evidence that our thoughts can have an effect upon plants from thousands of miles away. A summarized version of this experiment is as follows: Marcel had a laboratory filled with plants hooked up to EEG (Electroencephalograph) equipment and strip-graph recorders. The object of the experiment was to see if his thoughts of love and light projected from thousands of miles away to these plants could reach them. He was scheduled to give a lecture in Prague, Czechoslovakia. His assistant was told to monitor the plants and that when Vogel got to Prague, he would determine what time of day he would send these thoughts of love and light to these plants. In other words, a double-blind scientific method experiment was set up. When he got to Prague, some 10,000 miles away, he decided to send the thoughts of love and light to the plants exactly at 6:00 P.M. Prague time for five days straight. This is exactly what he did, though he did fall asleep one of the nights at the designated time and was unable to transmit the thought. Each time his intention was to send love from his heart and light from his brow center to his favorite plant in the laboratory 10,000 miles away.

When Vogel got back, he discovered that at exactly 6:00 P.M. Prague time, his favorite plant had responded first by eliciting micro-electromagnetic impulses to the electronic Whetstone-Bridge micro-response monitor , and subsequently the rest of the plants in the laboratory followed it's response. The plants had responded only four out of the five schedule times. The response time of the plants was instantaneous. The great distance seemed to make no difference with the objective. The results of these experiments have had incredible impact on what we believed to be true about the potential of human thought to travel great distances, as well as the response of plants to emotions. For extraordinary research on various realities within the plant kingdom, we suggest

The Secret Life Of Plants, by Tompkins and Bird.

Science cannot explain how thought and thought-forms work, nor can it explain the rationale of mental activity that transcends time and space. There are only suggestions and clues from the scientific community. According to T. Edward Ross, during the *"search,"* the dowser will register brainwaves including beta, alpha, theta, and delta on an electroencephalograph. All these brain waves will register on the electroencephalogram at the same time. The dowser is therefore considered to be in resonance with the Schumann Resonance of 8 plus Hertz, which is the "signature" of the earth. In other words, the act of dowsing reflects a full range of brainwave activity, and the whole system with all of its parts seems to be working together in an efficient functional balance which is consistent with the Earth's balanced energy.

Distance dowsing involves the ability to send one's Intuition to investigate a place, thing, or condition in question, and return to the sender the desired information. It is the vital life force of the dowser that is able to transport itself to any part of the world or known universe with the incredible speed of thought. It moves free of the physical body and is able to intuitively communicate with the dowser through the movements of the pendulum.

Another perspective as to how the Intuition is able to acquire unknown information in distant dowsing from maps, photographs and other objects, theorizes that rays are being emitted from the subject itself. It may be that emanations from a subject are trapped light waves or rays. As science cannot definitively explain how and why distance dowsing works, the potential dowser will need to come to his/her own conclusion on this matter.

If part of your belief system is still having a hard time with all of this, think about your ability to attune yourself, or to come into sympathetic resonance with something that is a few feet away. Now expand that level of awareness so that you can see that it makes absolutely *no* difference to your intuitive or dowsing abilities whether an object is a few feet away or thousands of miles away. Our energy system allows us to broadcast, receive, and transmit information in the same way as a radio or television works. The mind, with *intention* and focused *concentration*, is a tuning device that works like a radio receiver. The body is your antenna. By holding an image of the objective of your search, by formulating clear and specific intention, and by a clear and focused communication with your Intuition, you can connect with the object and access the information you want.

This intuitive aspect of ourselves has an ability to do a type of "reconnaissance" at places throughout the world that may be thousands of miles away from the physical body. A part of our mind, (the intuitive part) combines with the universal life force energy that is already at the area of the search. Why does this happen? Every area, every object or person has its own unique qualities. Everything vibrates at a specific frequency. This is why a *witness* is such value in dowsing. The *witness* acts as a vibration or frequency reference point held in the dowser's conscious mind. This, and the visual imagery of the map or photo, causes the Intuition to make a link to the location of the object or substance of the *search*. As with all forms of dowsing, it is a matter of establishing

137

the sympathetic resonance of like frequencies. When contact at the *search* or *find point* is made by the awareness of the Intuition, there seems to be an almost instantaneous response.

One of the best ways to assure your conscious mind that map and distance dowsing works is to have an experienced map dowser do a water vein(s) test of your property from a hundred or more miles away with a map, a pendulum, and, perhaps, a rock sample from the test area. Then at home, water-dowse the area yourself. You may come up with the same or similar results, proving to yourself that the "unknowns" can be realized without being in close proximity to the test area.

The next step is to do distance or map dowsing yourself on your or someone else's land so that you can easily check the accuracy of the results of your practice. As long as you can maintain a clear, concise, and accurate image or visualization of the object of the search, you do have the ability to use a part of your mind to link with something hundreds or thousands of miles away in a matter of seconds.

One of the most fascinating long distance or map dowsing cases involves a man by the name of Verne Cameron. In 1959, Verne Cameron contacted the United States Navy and told them that by using a map and a pendulum, he would be able to locate the entire submarine fleet. In March 1959, Vice Admiral Maurice Curtis wrote a letter to Mr. Cameron: *"I am advised you believe you may be able to tell the location of all the submarines in the world's water by a technique called " Map Dowsing." It is suggested you be given an opportunity to confirm your ability on the subject."* Soon after the letter, Cameron met with the Vice Admiral in Southern California and the rest of the Navy brass to demonstrate the technique. Within a few minutes Cameron located every single submarine, to the total amazement of those present. He also located every Russian submarine around the world. Despite the success of this test, Cameron did not hear from the Navy or United States Government until years later.

Cameron had been invited by the South African government to their country in order to discover various natural resources using his Intuition and a pendulum. When he applied for a passport, however, to his great surprise he was turned down. He investigated the reason for the denial and found that the Navy had contacted the C.I.A. about his submarine dowsing ability. The intelligence agency labelled him a security risk and would not allow him the freedom to travel outside the country for fear he might reveal top-secret military information.

Yet even the military evolves. During the Viet Nam conflict, Robert McNamara, then Secretary of Defense, used a pendulist to locate underground tunnels, land mines, and ammunition dumps. Today, we hope that the Intuition be used only in ways that will be much more peaceful.

Map and distance dowsing are easy methods for city and suburban dwellers to practice for developing their intuitive abilities. It is possible to sit in the comfort of your own home or apartment and dowse faraway places, or even a vacant lot down the street.

This method can be very helpful in finding the perfect house or piece of land to buy for you and your family.

For the last 25 years I have used this method for every home I have lived in. I first find the perfect time for the move, and then find the perfect location (specific area). I have always been amazed at how accurate this can be. I have dowsed the specific weekend to locate the perfect house and land to live in some 2 to 6 months in advance. This technique has allowed me to be the first to show up and to be chosen from a list of 25 or more applicants or buyers to rent or buy the most perfect house. My friends used to wonder how I obtained such great houses, perfect settings, ideal living conditions, and at a cost much lower than others of equal value!

Distant Dowsing Preparation

The ideal condition for map and long distance dowsing is at the time when your energy level is highest and when there is the least amount of noise and distraction. Do it only when you feel bright and energized. If it is a gloomy day and you are the type that can be drained by that type of weather, then wait for blue sky and sunshine, if that is what it takes. Some people find that late night is appropriate for them because of the great decrease in environmental noise and airwave activity from radio, television, and microwave transmission.

When dowsing with a map, you can use a simple hand-drawn map as well as purchased ones. Most black and white or colored maps, charts, diagrams, or photos will prove satisfactory. However, for accurate dowsing, remember that maps not drawn to scale can throw off the find by a distance of several feet to several miles. If your map is scaled too small, you will have difficulty in pinpointing precise areas. For this reason, we prefer a blown-up version of the concentrated area of the search, accompanied by a small scale map covering the surrounding region.

In map dowsing, you may be surprised at times to find your pointer directing itself off the edge of the map. In this case, the location sought may be found on an adjacent map, or by adding a blank sheet of paper. For instance, the course of an underground stream may easily be projected on the adjacent map, and it may be necessary to hand-draw the remaining section of stream on a piece of paper. Just follow the instrument and the pointer.

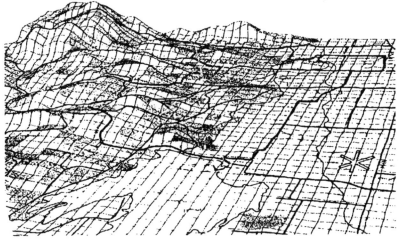

Topographical map with quadrant grid pattern.

Often, you may be dowsing a map that was previously dowsed by another person with similar *search* objectives. You will need to use some form to rule out, neutralize, or protect yourself from other existing thought-forms from the previous person's work. We have shared with you numerous methods of surrounding yourself and the object of the search with protective *light* through breath, affirmations, prayer and focused intention. Find a method that works for you so that you are not influenced by extraneous variables that may inhibit your effectiveness and use it whenever you work.

Preparation: It is important to prepare yourself mentally for map dowsing and to be specific in what you are looking for. BE ALERT for clues as you proceed, and your Intuition will guide the instrument in your hand and prompt you. Be prepared to record and evaluate your findings with the utmost thoroughness.

Now begin your line of questioning:

- "Is now the perfect time and place to be doing this search?"

- "Is it within my ability to find _____ (object of test)?"

- "Is it to my highest and greatest benefit to find _____ (name, substance, etc.)?"

- "I can find _____ (name, or substance) in this segment____ (Yes/No)?"

- "The probability of finding _____ (name, substance, etc., is what degree in this segment _____ (%)?"

- "My access to my Intuition regarding this subject is to what degree ___(%)"

Start by tuning in or getting a feel for both that which you want to find and the general area under consideration. Orient the map to true North-South. With a ruler, draw lines radiating out from a single point, subdividing the search area into smaller segments; this will look like a sunburst pattern. The single point that you choose as a starting point should be a point on the map that can be easily found, such as a landmark, river, surveyor marker, road marker, etc. Focus your mind on the object of the search while looking at a map of the general area. Free your mind of any preconceived ideas concerning the pendulum's movement as to where you might expect to find the objects of the search. Now, soft focus your eyes from the map by looking past or "through" the map using your peripheral vision to register the results of each test. This will help to keep your eyes from catching on one particular area for too long. Noticing one spot in particular may cause you to lose your concentration and possibly give you false results. Through your peripheral vision, watch for any exaggerated or excited action of the pendulum as the pointer moves over "live" areas on the map, photo, or diagram. Feel for these spots and remember to keep your thought continually on the quest for the person, place, or object sought. Be alert to any change in direction or swing of the pendulum as you proceed. With a wooden pointer, or the index finger of your left hand, point to each area.

Continue with this process until you have narrowed it down to a smaller area. Then get a "quadrant map" of that particular area and narrow it down again. From there work from the point of your radiating lines; make sure your map is oriented on true North, and begin working with your questions: "From this point, the object that I am seeking is what direction or degree from known point____?" Then draw a line from the point on the map in the direction or precise degree. Then ask: "I will find the object_____ within how many feet, yards, miles, from this point ____?" Now draw the intersecting line on your degree line. The *find point* is where the lines intersect. Now go and recheck your *find point* and see if results are accurate.

As with all dowsing, it is most important for the map dowser to remain neutral and objective to avoid a forced or contrived situation. One's ego can nullify map dowsing success. It is better to map- dowse in a surrendered, objective state of mind, employing the Intuition with confidence. Avoid the urge to find correct answers without first giving your Intuition ample time to investigate and evaluate the situation. Some of the greatest locating failures have been caused by not realizing that a few moments of concentrated thought imagery backed with desire (wishful thinking) can make a totally false location look like a genuine find. We highly recommend that you refrain from making up your mind about the results as you would like them to be. Unfortunately, you can create a positive thought picture so vividly in your mind that the person, object, or substance seems to be there. The active subconscious mind can at times work in such a way that you delude yourself. This does not mean that the subconscious has malicious intent. However, the subconscious is that part of the mind without reasoning ability; it does wish to please and can exaggerate to do so. It is best not to concentrate on *where* a certain person, object or substance must be. By doing so, you can create a false thought image and transpose its reaction through your instrument. The dowsing device in your hand cannot differentiate; it can follow this influence and be led to a false site. This problem has, on more than one occasion, shaken an individual's confidence in map dowsing.

As always, before investing a great deal of time and money in planning around a *find point*, do go and check it out. Be alert to wishful thinking and visions of grandeur. Use as many ways as possible for checking out a particular *find point*. Sometimes the Intuition will take you to a *find point* to show you something else that you need to know, or something you may have overlooked in your preliminary test. Using a combination of intuitive tools such as subtle-sensing, pendulum, and dowsing rods can be helpful as a way of verifying your test results. In other cases, it would also be advisable (before digging some 30 feet in attempt to find a buried treasure chest) to bring in other tools such as a quality metal detector or other means of verification.

If you continue your questioning once you located the *find point*, you could ask: "I will find this object _____ located _____ (how many inches, feet, etc.) below the surface _____?" Now you may have found your treasure, though I would like to caution you on treasure hunts. These methods *can* work on treasure hunts and you can be successful. However, I have seen some dowsers taken down the yellow brick road of illusion because of emotional investment in the outcome. To use the Intuition and the pendulum with accuracy, one does need to be careful about appropriately using his abilities for capital gain.

Problem Solving—House

Distance dowsing can be an incredible tool for intuitive problem-solving. An interesting application of a long-distance dowsing happened some years ago when I had my construction business. I was working on a complete remodeling of a house, and for some inexplicable reason, the customer lost electricity to half of the kitchen. The electrical subcontractor spent two days tracing down every possible cause and found nothing. Another electrician was called in who also found it to be a mystery. They were ready to wire in a whole new line and bypass the old one. Meanwhile, I took Polaroid photos of the house; I went home that night and spent about one-half hour doing a long distance photo test. I determined that on the front side of the house by the left side of the kitchen patio door, in the second panel to the left and the sixth nail over we would find the cause. The next day, I discreetly told my customer and the subcontractor what I found, and of course they looked at me as if I were crazy. I could tell they were not going to act on the information I had given them. So I said that I would pull the wood paneling off myself, on my time and expense, and have a look. Meanwhile, I was thinking, "I sure hope I'm right, because this could look pretty bad if I'm not!" What I discovered when I pulled off the wood paneling was that, sure enough, the sixth nail over had severed one side of the electrical line. Everyone thought it was great that the problem was solved, but even to this day I bet they think the procedure in finding the solution was a little crazy. I quickly played the story down, for it was definitely beyond their comprehension.

There are four messages in this story for you. First, there was a definite need. Secondly, we do know how to determine the unknown from a photo over long distance, and third, these techniques work best when you keep the ego out of the way and do not try to impress anyone with your abilities, and fourth, not everyone is able to talk about, understand or process what your work as a pendulist is about and it may be best to keep a low profile.

The following is a form of distance dowsing that you can apply to your own house or a house you plan on buying or renting for yourself or others. A photo or plans of the house will do just fine as a witness.

House Inventory:

Dowsing Report on: _____

Date _____

A. Roof:
Shingles/Slates: do they need replacing in next years.

> If damaged, where? _____
> Metal flashing (needed): ____ any leaks or other potential problems _____
> If so, where _____
> Gutters: _____adequate _____
>> problems _____ where _____
> Downspouts: problems __ where _____
> Rafters & Braces: any problems _____
>> where _____
> Soffits: _____ good repair & adequate

> if not, where _____
> Ventilation: is this adequate under roof _____

B. Insulation:

Ceiling: _____ is it adequate

if not, above which rooms _____

Walls: is it adequate _____

if not, where _____

Basement: is it adequate _____

If not, where _____

C. Exterior Walls:

Brick: are there cracks _____

where _____

Is pointing required _____ where _____

leaning or bulging_____

Stucco: does it need repair _ where _____

Is it solidly affixed _____

Siding: needs repair need painting/stain _____

Caulking: need around windows _____

around doors_____

D. Entrances:

Doors: is insulation O.K. _____

are they hung properly_____

are locks secure _____

are there screens _____

Windows: are frames O.K. _____

do they fit O.K. _____

do they need painting _____

are they burglarproof _____

need of caulk _____

are there screens _____

E. Heating:

Furnace:_____

does it need replacing in next _____ year/s.

Piping: if hot water, are there leaks _____

is there corrosion _____
If hot air, is system operating _____
O.K. _____
is humidity system O.K. _____
is dehumidifying system,
    or air purification system working properly
Fireplace/Woodstove: are they in good order ___
does internal masonry in chimney require repair_
  does external chimney require repair _____
  is there a good draft_____
  any smoke-leaks out into room or under roof _

F. Basement:
  any structural defects _____
  any damp spots _____ where _____
  adequate height _____ water leaks _____

G. Sewers:_____
Septic: problems inside house _____
  outside_____
Storm: problems inside (such as backing up) _____
  problems outside, perimeter drains _____
  storm drain outflow _____

H. Electrical:
Service: properly fixed to house _____
  adequate rating for house (amps)_____
Fusing: is house fitted with adequate fuses or
circuit breakers _____
Wiring: correct type/rating _____
Fixtures: are lighting fixtures and wall outlets safe
  if not, where _____

I. Gas/Oil:
  if any, are these supplies in good workingorder

J. Grounds:
Garden: are there fencing problems _____

where _____

any unsafe trees/shrubs where _____

toxic substances in grounds _____

where _____

major pest problems_____

Driveways: _____

is surfacing adequate____ problems_____

Garage:_____ sound in structure__ doors fit

roof O.K._____

K. General:

Is area liable to flooding _ earthquakes _____

possible zoning changes in next 5/10 years ___

possible development of area in next 5/10 years

possible impact of development _____

of new highways in next 5/10 years _____

Is property close to High Voltage transmission

lines _____

are there any "noxious rays"

running under or through house _____

caused by "streams" electromagnetic_____

transmission _____ ore bodies_____

Should You Make This Investment _____

In order to undertake this survey, all that is required
is a floor plan of the house, or a photo of house. Set
the plans and/or photos and map of the area in
alignment with compass directions. Begin to access a
'feel' of the house and location. Visualize it in your
mind with as much detail as possible. When you
have felt or seen the entire picture, begin your house
inventory.

Dowsing Photographs

You can apply your intuitive or dowsing abilities to a photo of person(s), places(s), objects(s), or substances(s), living, dead, or inanimate as though they were in your immediate presence. You can determine the sex of the individual, or know whether he or she is living at the moment the picture is dowsed. Even if the photo is obscured, the present location of the person as he/she moves from one place to another can be determined.

All that is needed to do distant photo dowsing is a pendulum, *Pendulum Charts*-if you have them-a photo of the person, place or object of the *search*, and your faith and determination that this is within your abilities. When using a photo in testing a person, make sure that there is no one else or any animal in the photo with the person being tested. It does not matter how old the photo is; its only purpose is to help you to tune into the frequency of that person, place, or animal.

Before you start, *always* surround yourself and the person of the inquiry with the *White Light and Love*, and ask, for example, "Infinite Spirit or Infinite Intelligence, allow me now to be tuned into this person. Is it to this person's highest and greatest benefit for me to do this test?" "Is it of this person's will for me to do this test and do I have their permission?" "Let this be of thy will and not my will." Only continue if the pendulum answers are a resounding *Yes*. If the pendulums answers Yes gyration **DO NOT** continue on. As with everything in life there is a fine line between balance and imbalance, to any of this line of inquiry are anything but a strong Yes gyration **DO NOT** continue. As with everything in life there is a fine line between balance and imbalance, light and dark, the good and the bad. You <u>do not</u> want to cross the line no matter how tempted you may be, for the outcome would not be for either your, or the other person's, highest benefit. Continuing could potentially hurt you or them in the long run. With a *Yes* answer, you have permission to continue checking on all the various aspects and attributes of the physical, mental, emotional and etheric bodies.

Dowsing Photographs: First place your left hand above the photo. Slowly raise and lower your palm; meanwhile 'sense' the energy focal point (the highest level of intensity) above the picture. Mentally pose one question at a time: "Is the subject in the photo now alive? Traveling? Married?" etc. Swing your pendulum and await the *Yes, No, Maybe,* or *More-Or-Less* response.

Locating Loved Ones

You can use this technique to locate loved ones from whom you may be separated. First of all, it helps to know a little information about the person being sought. It also helps to define exactly whom you are seeking. A name may not necessarily be enough. If the parents are asking for the information, then state your request as follows: I am seeking the physical location of the individual known as Mary Jane Smith, born May 23, 1969, who was living at .....address...., the daughter of John and Sue Smith, 244 Main St. Podunk, Iowa. "Infinite, may I locate this particular individual?", "Can I locate this particular individual?", "Should I locate this particular individual?", "Am I now ready?" Proceed only if you receive *Yes* answers.

Your job will be easier if you have several maps and some yardsticks available. When looking for the location of a person for the first time without any clues, it is best to start with a world map. Begin the search with a world map, then continue with a regional map, and then finish with a local map with the top of the map orientated to true North. Then ask "Infinite, please indicate on this map the location of the individual I am searching for at this point in time." The pendulum will swing to point in a given direction across the map. When the motion has stabilized in one particular direction, gently lay a ruler or yardstick down in that precise direction. Go to another side and ask the same question. Then again with the third side, and finally the fourth side. The intersection of all the yardsticks will give you an exact location. Place a mark on the map at the spot. Then switch to a regional map of the indicated area and repeat the process. You can continue to use more detailed maps until you can locate the individual in a particular building on a particular street! It helps to write in the date and time by each of the marks on each of the maps. Dowsing daily or weekly will add confidence to your dowsing skill and also will indicate the path of the individual, Using the marked map, you will be able to check the accuracy of your dowsing at a later time.

Missing Person Search

Never volunteer! Always wait to be asked. If this is an area where you feel you can be of service I suggest that you work with missing persons you hear about, follow the news, go through the steps, and watch the outcome.

How do you establish credibility? Set up search situations to test your ability, and when you begin to see consistent accuracy, contact the appropriate Search and Rescue groups and explain to them how you will attempt to assist them.

When you have been called in to participate in a search and rescue, prepare yourself for some apprehension from those in the group. Start your work by collecting as much information as you can about the missing party. If a picture will aid you, get it. Where was the person last seen, by whom, when, what were the intentions (if known) of the individual at that time, what are the habits as they pertain to the disappearance? Feed all this into your mind-computer so that you have a sense of the missing person as completely as possible.

Seclude yourself if you work best alone, or have a second person to help you with the first steps of Map Dowsing. Get detailed maps of the area. If you are looking in a city, get a block-by-block map; if the country, a geodetic topographic type; if the person has traveled you may need state or regional maps. As for the actual procedure, use the previous methodology *Locating Loved Ones*, or earlier in the book, Direction-Finding.

Of all of the dowsing methods, distant and map dowsing may be the most difficult to comprehend and believe in. Whatever applications you intend to use these techniques for, practice will enhance your confidence and your ability. Your preconceptions and beliefs may be deeply rooted, so be patient.

Also consider that in some cases knowledge can be a terrible burden. Do not ask for information that you would rather not know or that you do not need to know! Ask what the knowledge might cost you. Not all missing persons are found, and some of the cases are terribly tragic. Could you handle this if such were the case?

As with all types of dowsing, work to neutralize your ego involvement. Humility can go a long way in assisting your practice and results. It is always important to ask permission to dowse and to surround yourself and the person or object of the search in the *White Light and Love* (see Chapter 4). It is especially important in distant and map dowsing so that you not interfere with the desires, lessons, or free will of the person for whom you are searching.

Chapter 9

Challenges to Successful Form

Most people learning the skills to access the Intuition will find themselves, along the line somewhere, having to deal with errors, and setbacks at various points in their dowsing development. In the beginning, for some, everything seems to work smoothly and easily. Then for some, to their surprise, everything appears to go wrong and nothing seems to work. If you find yourself with this challenge, you may be asking, "What happened?" The state of, "Why doesn't this work right any more?" is just a part of the learning process. Then comes the work and determination to build the discipline to make it into a usable skill that will last.

However, the frequency of error reduces with time as the dowser gains experience and as he/she becomes clearer of mental, emotional and physical interferences. An understanding of the reasons for dowsing errors can help veterans as well as amateurs to avoid repeating the same mistakes. Often we tend to focus on successful experiences rather than finding the cause of our errors. In this work, the influences of these dowsing mishaps or failures are being labeled 'jeopardy influences' and have been divided into levels associated with the various aspects of our consciousness. Jeopardy influences are potential problems or stumbling blocks that you may run into on your journey into proficient dowsing.

Jeopardy influences are internal or external conditions that can become obstacles to effective results. A protective light energy field may keep one relatively clear in spite of the presence of several of these *jeopardy influences*. A dowser may even have enough energy to override the conflicting influence of certain *jeopardy influences*. Yet it is possible that the existence of even one *jeopardy influence* can cause some degree of interference and affect accuracy. The point is that it is important to be aware of these *jeopardy influences*. By being consciously aware of them, the dowser can work to control, clear, or neutralize the influences as much as possible. *Jeopardy influences* are of various types and may be grouped according to physical, mental, emotional, and psychic/spiritual sources.

Being aware of the following jeopardy influences will help you to know what problematic situations and circumstances to avoid. Most of you have experienced the slight difference between the *feel* of right answers, the *feel* of wrong answers and when you are really not sure. This is why we need to monitor ourselves all the time. It is only by watching our thoughts and feelings as we work that we know when things are not what they should be and what *jeopardy influences* are affecting our results.

Dowsing Inventory of Jeopardy Influences

Physical Internal Influences:

☐ Hunger and/or fatigue

☐ Improper diet, poor nutrition, or gluttony

☐ Vitamin and mineral deficiency

- [ ] Infection, illness, disease, and trauma

- [ ] Chemical/pH/hormonal/glandular imbalance

- [ ] Drug use of all kinds, including caffeine, tobacco, alcohol, and medications

Physical External Influences:

- [ ] Electrical or electromagnetic fields

- [ ] Audio and/or visual distractions or disturbances

- [ ] Noxious negative earth energies

- [ ] Weather disturbances, full moon, sun spots

- [ ] Threats to physical safety, insecurity, stress

- [ ] Dirty, smelly, or otherwise offensive surroundings or environment

- [ ] Lack of sacred or psychic space

Mental Internal Influences:

- [ ] Depression, anxiety, and stress

- [ ] High expectations, wishful thinking

- [ ] Addictions, obsessions, compulsions, and perversions

- [ ] Projection, denial, and other defense mechanisms

- [ ] Intellectual conceit, egotism, and vanity

- [ ] Disbelief, doubt, fear of higher levels of consciousness

☐ Desire to control, reactionary thoughts, self-pity, self-doubt, selfish motive

☐ Negative thought patterns including judgment, greed, self-centeredness, and others

☐ Biased interpretation of response because of limited belief system

☐ Lack of focus or concentration

Mental External Influences:

☐ Subliminal messages

☐ Hypnotic domination

☐ Violent movies/films, books/magazines

☐ Psionic devices

Emotional Internal Influences:

☐ Emotional attachment to the answer, i.e., strong aversion or wishful thinking

☐ Limitations regarding how much information you can handle at the time

☐ Undisciplined emotions: fear, anger, doubt, jealously, guilt, hate, rage, envy, hostility, resentment, dissension, unforgiving, worry

☐ Emotionally painful or embarrassing information which the subconscious mind may withhold or exaggerate

☐ Traumatic memories (especially sexual abuse/ molestation) which may cause the subconscious to cover up

☐ Fear of or resistance to the answer

Emotional External Influences:

☐ Abuse of all kinds

☐ Experience of injustice, violation, abandonment

☐ Withholding love

Psychic/Spiritual Influences:

☐ Unbalanced chakras

☐ External Influences

☐ Presence of skeptics

☐ Entities in the auric field

☐ Locations such as graveyards

☐ Sites of traumatic incidents, such as murder or rape

☐ Psychic attack, either by conscious or unconscious

☐ Season or time of year, time of lunar cycle, negative astrological influence

☐ Empathetic or sympathetic pains (picking up another's suffering)

☐ Psychic intrusion by disharmonious forces: human earthbound discarnates, nonhuman entities, fallen angels, devils, satanics and demonics, elementals, thought-forms, evil adepts and masters of sorcery, jealous and manipulative "gurus," and occasionally, animals.

Knowing about these potential interferences can assist you in sorting through possible influences in your process of development. Physiological factors are more easily dowsed for by yourself. Mental and emotional influences, on the other hand, are more difficult, and sometimes better checked by another. This most often is because of the difficulty in relation to remaining objective in the answer or outcome. Psychic and spiritual influences are by far the greatest problems to recognize and may also require the assistance of another dowser to determine the existence of such disharmonious presences.

Accessibility to the Intuition

We have looked at the various aspects and attributes that can hinder effective and accurate results with the answers we receive. What we have been labeling as jeopardy influences is nothing more than *resistance* of the subconscious to allow full access of the Intuition. The information, knowledge, or wisdom at any given moment from the Intuition is in fact always right, true, accurate or correct. The Intuition itself does have total access to the Infinite All Knowing.

The most important facet of this entire chapter or perhaps the most important consideration in all pendulum work is knowing to what degree resistance or jeopardy influences are in the way of accessing the Intuition. It would be of great value to you, whether or not you're a beginner or advanced student, to measure your accessibility percentage to the subject of inquiry. This is especially true if you know you may have some emotional charge around the subject or if you get a subtle-sense that your answers just don't feel quite right.   If this is the case, we would strongly suggest asking; "Infinite, what is my accessibility to the Intuition at this time ____(%)?," and "To what degree is my resistance to the truths, information, etc. at this time____(%)?" This can be extremely helpful in determining the degree of accuracy of the information. This query can be a great gift in helping you to see what areas of your life need attention and healing and to clear the issues or unresolved emotional charge behind the resistance. This information is invaluable not only in knowing yourself better but most of all, to help you become a whole, healthy and complete individual who is able to fulfill most if not all of your desires. Keep in mind, the subconscious does *not* have an agenda to do you wrong, malicious intent or anything of the like. I believe subconscious resistance to influence total accessibility to the Intuition is only intended to present an opportunity to bring to the light any and all areas of one's life experience that have not completely been dealt with. All this is so that we can find our way to health, happiness and total well-being. The resistance is not a negative, but a gift as the doorway through to well-being.

The lack of truth or an untrue answer can come from the subconscious mind. Although it can appear deceiving, the purpose of an untruth is not malicious. This may happen in the interest of your protection if you seek information which you are not mentally or emotionally prepared to hear. It may be that your subconscious is trying to keep covered particular traumatic memories.

The other part to this subconscious intervention may be the result of a long-standing pattern involving various charged issues that the subconscious may have an investment in. For example, if there is a long lineage of lack around money, and the emotional agenda has not been healed and cleared, the potential for success in accessing the winning lottery numbers may be limited. It doesn't mean that we don't attempt to do something that we are drawn to, it just may be that we need to do some emotional or mental house cleaning first in order for success to prevail.

Wrong answers may result from asking out of wrong or selfish motives, or asking for trivial information. Proper motivation means that the dowser is coming from a place of true need, is sincere, and has the highest good of all concerned at heart. Furthermore, the Intuition may give distorted information when it detects mistrust, skepticism, testing, or lack of respect on the part of the dowser. The appropriate attitude is crucial, even in the observer, before the dowser can receive reliable results.

Solutions

Of course, we would not just give you the problem without offering workable solutions. There are many ways for healing and clearing subconscious blocks, traumatic imprints, possessions, or psychic intrusions. The forms of therapy associated with such dis-orders and dysfunctions are beyond the scope of this book. Nonetheless, there are some forms of transformational therapy that we have seen to be most effective in restoration of one's total well-being. This approach involves naming a specific problem area and dowsing to determine the number of reasons contributing to the dysfunction. The following list of categories, or "keys" to assist you in identifying the reasons, purpose, or awareness for various conscious or subconscious negative programs. See pendulum charts: *Personal Motivators, What Is Going On, Who Is Involved, What Am I Telling Myself, How to Change My Life and Healing Remedies.*

The Identification Keys:

☐ Life Experiences

☐ Past Trauma Imprint

☐ Mental Patterns

☐ Emotional Patterns

☐ Family Lineage Patterns

☐ Childhood Patterns

☐ Past Life Residue

☐ Disincarnates/Entities/Thought Forms

Once identified, the negative conditioning or imprints can be cleared by the appropriate affirmations, prayer, and therapy. However, each condition or imprint cleared or neutralized must immediately be programmed with a positive program, condition, or energy. You must literally fill that space which the negative conditioning occupied. (Affirmations are particularly good for this.) Review chapter 4 and 5 for some ways to remedy negative conditioning. Your pendulum and pendulum charts can assist you in determining therapy modalities to use, and an appropriate time to use them.

Negativity of any kind will cause pollution within our environment, our beings and also within our bodies. Awareness and protection are the keys to success against *jeopardy influences.* Denial, blame, or martyrdom will not bring success on any level in overcoming these stumbling blocks.

No matter how detrimental a possession or entity may seem, we must always ask permission first before releasing disincarnates. "Some people have accepted discarnates as a part of the learning and overcoming program they established for themselves to challenge them in this life, and (we) have no right to interfere." [2] In some circumstances, the discarnates may have set up a situation, with the permission of the host, in order to learn certain lessons without having to incarnate. Even in the case of nonhuman entities, one must be aware that "some people want to keep the possession in order to feel special or powerful." [3]

Accurate information about the future, as previously discussed, is the most difficult to obtain from the Intuition. The ego will sometimes manipulate the future once it is known, against its own best interest. This may be the result of some subconscious self-sabotage or self-punishment programs or conditioning.

Having some awareness and knowledge of the nature of spiritual guides can be most helpful in forming realistic conceptions of them. Guides can come from many different dimensions, realities, forms, and planes of existence. Their expertise is equally as varied as is their level of proficiency in connecting with humans. They also can have limitations and be at different stages of their own evolution. What is important, and this is perfectly clear, is that they be of the Light. Guides at higher levels of awareness can be recognized by their attempts to help you empower yourself. If they are truly your guides, they will assist you in remembering who you are, to let go of fear, and to love yourself and others. Highly-evolved guides will encourage your independence and self-sufficiency. They will assist your decisions, but they will not make them for you. Rather, they will point you in the appropriate direction. Spiritually-evolved guides will encourage you to trust your own Intuition. Rarely will guides predict future events, for they are careful not to take away your lessons. Their messages are positive and uplifting, expressing truths in precise, and almost simple, terms. Yet, they are humble and will admit their word is not absolute.

The lower level guides, by contrast, are pretentious and talk in profound sounding trivialities. Most often they lack greater understanding and genuine wisdom. Usually they are attracted by one's curiosity. They like to stir up emotions by predicting disastrous events, or to flatter people's egos with grandiose predictions. Low level guides like to entice one into giving power to them and one is usually left feeling fearful or depressed. Somehow outright offensive misbehavior with no commitment at all to spiritual growth or to one's highest and greatest benefit. Keeping as free as possible of *jeopardy influences* is the best insurance for not attracting them in the first place.

If there is the least question in your mind of interfering *jeopardy influences*, always check to see if additional protection is needed. Even after all *jeopardy influences* are eliminated, there is still the possibility of error due to improper procedure.

Errors Due to Procedure

☐ Lack of focus or concentration.

☐ Not checking to see if clearing, balancing, or protection is needed.

☐ Failing to determine the identity of where the source of information comes from.

☐ Neglecting to ask the questions Can I? May I? Should I? Am I Ready?

☐ Failing to check for interferences arising during the search.

☐ Doubt, lack of trust or respect for the source, testing the source.

☐ Incorrect motivation, lack of true need.

☐ Lack of specificity in asking the question, incorrect wording.

☐ Not checking for emotional or mental interference with the answers.

☐ Incorrect interpretation of response.

☐ Not checking accessibility percentage

In summary, the preparation of the dowser begins with the proper attitude of faith, trust, respect, and a sincere motivation based on true need. The most common error is the lack of being specific in asking the question, or incorrect wording of the question. Usually this error has to do with not being specific enough about time and place, or about the language with your pendulum. Keep in mind that the subconscious mind takes everything totally literally. One should take care to define to the subconscious which reality you are directing your line of questioning to: the actual physical reality or that which is imagined, potential, alternate, or subjective.

Remember, the pendulum tool provides a means of focus; a precise and narrow place to focus your attention: but the actual work is done by observing, by being aware, being wide open to all possibilities.

Finally, learn how to protect yourself from mental, emotional, and physical interference. Asking if you can does not always mean that you will avoid interference, or resistance to accessibility and that some precautionary steps may be needed before you proceed. Lower thoughts and negative emotions must be kept to a minimum and transformed toward the higher mental and emotional realms.

By doing your work to enhance your personal growth, you will be paving the way for clearing out negativity. Reestablishing positive patterns where the negativity once was will assist you in your personal growth, will help to minimize *jeopardy influences*, and increase quality of living.

Errors and mistakes may still occur, but we can make them our friends...our teachers. *We can learn more from our mistakes than we can from our successes.*

[1] Detzler, Robert E., 1988, Your Mind Net
[2] Detzler, Robert E., 1988: p242, Your Mind Net
[3] Greene, Linda L., 1990: p64, Learning the Secret Language

Chapter 10
What You Can Learn From Others

In this chapter you have the opportunity to experience many people's efforts in becoming proficient in the skills of using the pendulum. The following questionnaire was sent out to the American Society of Dowsers chapters throughout the country. The questionnaire was a fill-in-the-blank type designed to inspire creative input with attention to issues, difficulties and solutions. You will find some overlapping of information in the answers that were provided. The dots behind each subject represent an individual who directly addressed that subject. Had the questionnaire been a multiple choice, I'm sure the response would have been quite different; many more dots would have been checked off behind the subjects provided. Nonetheless, you may find that in the way in which people responded regarding the applications for which the pendulum can be used, what issues arose, and what challenges and solutions came forth to be insightful. From a cross section of fifty individuals and a composite of thousands of hours of pendulum practice you will see the ways in which others work. From the questionnaire provided you may find insight into your own unique approach as you use the pendulum, what frustrations you may need to grow beyond, and the challenges that you may encounter.

Throughout this book we have attempted to give you a broad approach to the pendulum. As one dowser so clearly states it, "Each individual must search for what works best for them. There is no universal way to dowse." "One single way for all people is not feasible." "Countless teachers are dogmatic that "their way" is the best way.---(Wrong!) Practice, Practice, Practice." -----Ross Dedrickson, WA. We encourage you to take the time to study this research because you can learn a great deal from others which in turn can save you a lot of time in your learning process.

Pendulum Dowsers Questionnaire

Quantity of questionnaires = 54
◆◆◆◆◆◆◆◆◆◆◆◆◆◆◆◆◆◆◆◆◆◆◆◆◆◆◆◆
◆◆◆◆◆◆◆◆◆◆◆◆◆◆◆◆◆◆◆◆◆◆◆◆◆◆◆◆

How long have you been using a pendulum?
1-2 years: ◆◆
2-3 years: ◆◆◆◆◆◆◆◆◆
4-7 years: ◆◆◆◆◆◆◆◆◆◆◆◆◆◆◆◆◆
8-14 years: ◆◆◆◆◆
15-20 years: ◆◆◆◆◆◆◆◆
25-30 years: ◆◆◆◆◆◆

How long did it take before you felt proficient in using a pendulum?
1 hour: ◆◆◆
few days: ◆
few weeks: ◆◆◆◆◆◆◆◆◆◆◆
2-6 months: ◆◆◆◆◆◆◆◆◆◆◆
1 year: ◆◆◆◆◆◆◆
2-3 years: ◆◆◆◆◆◆
5 years: ◆◆◆
6+ years: ◆◆
once I programmed it: ◆
not yet: ◆◆◆

To what degree would you consider your answers to be accurate?
50-60%: ◆
60-70%: ◆◆◆◆◆◆
75-80%: ◆◆◆◆◆◆◆◆◆◆◆
85-90%: ◆◆◆◆◆◆◆◆◆◆
90-99%: ◆◆◆◆◆◆◆◆◆◆◆◆◆◆◆◆◆
100%: ◆◆◆◆◆
Don't know: ◆

To what degree do you trust the answers that you get with your pendulum?
50-60%: ◆
65-70%: ◆◆◆
75-80%: ◆◆◆◆◆◆◆◆
85-90%: ◆◆◆◆◆◆◆◆
90-95%: ◆◆◆◆◆◆◆◆◆◆◆◆◆
up to 100%: ◆◆◆◆◆◆◆◆◆◆◆◆◆◆◆◆◆◆◆◆

For what subjects, issues, or circumstances do you use your pendulum?

Any and all issues/circumstances one can think of, anything of importance: ◆◆◆◆◆◆◆◆◆◆◆◆
Animals, health problems, communications, finding farm animals: ◆◆◆◆◆◆
Astrology: ◆
Auras: ◆◆
Automobile diagnosing, repair: ◆◆◆◆◆◆◆
Business decisions, job estimates, high/low of what consumer will pay: ◆◆◆
Basic needs: ◆◆
Classes to take, courses to pursue: ◆◆◆
Checking and clearing entities: ◆◆◆
Compatabilities: ◆
Confirmation of others: ◆
Decisions, special decisions, helping to make up my mind: ◆◆◆◆◆◆◆◆◆◆◆

Directions: ◆◆◆

Earth Energies, earth changes, earthquakes, geopathic, noxious energies, EMF fields, chemicals: ◆◆◆◆◆◆◆◆◆◆◆◆ ◆◆◆◆◆◆◆

Energy displacement, changes (+/-), polarity of objects: ◆◆◆◆

Family, family issues: ◆◆

Financial, stockmarket, bookkeeping: ◆◆◆◆

Finding lost objects myself: ◆◆◆

Finding lost objects of others: ◆

Fishing spots: ◆

Food decisions, compatibility, supplements, food combinations, restaurants, diets, nutritional analysis, sprays (pesticides/herbicides/radiation):◆◆◆◆◆◆◆◆◆◆◆◆◆ ◆◆◆◆◆ ◆◆◆◆◆◆◆◆

Friends questions, for others: ◆◆◆◆◆◆◆

Health; issues, conditions, bodywork, blockages, physical, mental, emotional, energetic, etheric, anything that goes into my body, therapy, for others:◆◆◆◆◆◆◆◆◆◆◆◆◆◆◆ ◆◆◆◆◆◆ ◆◆◆◆◆◆◆◆◆◆◆◆

Healing: ◆◆◆◆◆◆◆◆◆◆◆◆◆

Homeopathics, herbs, flower essences, essential oils, gem essences, massage oils, herbal bath teas, colors, aromathrapy, radionics, cell/tissue salts: ◆◆◆◆◆◆◆◆◆◆◆◆◆◆

Household energies: ◆◆◆

Job opportunities, career: ◆◆

Judgement, purpose: ◆

Life's crossroads: ◆

Lost objects: ◆◆◆◆◆◆◆◆◆◆◆◆◆◆

Map dowsing: ◆◆◆◆◆◆◆◆◆

Medical decisions, directions, medicine, dosages, doctors: ◆◆◆◆◆◆◆◆

Missing person: ◆◆◆

Negative thought, spirits, fields: ◆◆◆

Personal issues, personal life, personal well being: ◆◆◆◆◆◆◆

Photos: ◆

Plant, soil-nutrients, agricultual, seeds: ◆◆◆◆◆◆

Psychological issues: ◆

Purchases: ◆◆◆◆◆◆◆◆

Purchasing vehicles: ◆
Reincarnation, past lives: ◆◆
Rental tenants: ◆
Scheduling work day, business: ◆◆
Serious questions, problems: ◆
Social issues, situations: ◆
Spiritual issues: ◆
Teaching others: ◆◆◆
Thought forms: ◆
Travel, best day, best areas, places to stay: ◆◆◆◆
Treasure: ◆◆
Vacation routes: ◆◆◆
Vitamins, food supplements: ◆◆◆◆◆◆◆◆◆◆◆◆◆◆
Water locations, purity, wells: ◆◆◆◆◆◆◆◆◆◆◆◆◆◆◆◆◆◆
Weather conditions, future weather conditions: ◆◆◆◆◆

With what subjects, issues, or circumstances have you had the most acurate results or success?
All: ◆◆◆◆◆◆◆◆◆
Anything not concerning myself: ◆
Astrology: ◆
Best travel days: ◆◆◆◆◆
Bodywork: ◆◆
Business problems, decisions: ◆◆◆◆◆
Buying gifts: ◆◆
Career decisions: ◆
Clearing; deceased releatives energy, directions, blocks to health etc.: ◆◆◆
Difficult decisions: ◆◆
Emotional, psychological issues: ◆
Essential oils, aromatherapy: ◆
Family decisions, condition of members: ◆◆◆
Food, supplements, dietary analysis, nutritional, vitamins: ◆◆◆◆◆◆◆◆◆◆◆◆
Geopathic zones: ◆◆◆
Happiness, well being:◆ ◆◆
Health problems, issues, physical problems/ailments:◆◆◆◆ ◆◆◆◆◆◆◆◆◆◆◆◆◆◆◆◆

Healing; body polarity, flower essences, spiritual response therapy: ◆◆◆◆◆◆◆
Helping others: ◆
House repair, diagnosis: ◆◆
Lost objects: ◆◆◆◆
Lost animals: ◆◆◆◆
Map dowsing: ◆◆◆◆◆
Noxious energies, rays, EFM fields, house energies, blocked energies: ◆◆◆◆◆◆◆
Nutrition: ◆◆◆◆◆◆
Personal Problems: ◆◆
Police cars- unmarked: ◆
Sex of unborn children: ◆
Spiritual issues: ◆
Thought forms: ◆
Water locations, purity, wells: ◆◆◆◆◆◆◆◆◆◆◆◆
Weather conditions: ◆◆

To what would you attribute this accuracy or success ?

Acknowledgement of Source, polite, Intuitive mind, becoming one with high self, tuning into universal mind, aligning to higher self through spoken word, listening to your guides: ◆◆◆◆◆◆◆◆◆◆◆◆
Asking the right questions: ◆◆◆◆◆◆◆◆
Careful wording, detailed, specific phrasing of questions, way the question is asked, right sequence of questions: ◆◆◆◆◆◆◆◆◆◆
Check for blocks, check all answers for accuracy: ◆
Concentration, focus, focusing intention: ◆◆◆◆◆◆◆◆◆◆
Confidence: ◆
Detachment to outcome, impersonality: ◆◆◆
Desire, wanting to know, need for correct results: ◆◆◆◆
Experience, knowledge: ◆ ◆
Faith, trust:, beliefs, trusting dowsing system: ◆◆◆◆◆◆
Helping others, others needs, being of service: ◆◆◆◆◆◆◆
Heritage, family lineage, naturally inclined, astrological: ◆◆◆◆

Honest need of good answers: ◆◆
Interpret results correctly: ◆
Learn from others: ◆
Listening and accepting the answers, sensitivity: ◆◆◆◆
Objectivity, openmindedness: ◆◆◆◆◆
Persistence, Practice, Perserverence, practice in the field: ◆◆◆◆
◆◆◆◆◆◆◆
Preparation, meditation, prayer, quiet time: ◆◆◆◆◆
Keeping Clear, clear minded, centered, balanced, calm, relaxed:
◆◆◆◆◆◆
Resonance with target: ◆
Relationship between myself, intuitive skills and the value of
my work: ◆
Senstivity expressed through movement of pendulum: ◆
Skill: ◆
Unselfishness, desire for the highest and greatest good of
others: ◆◆◆◆◆◆◆◆◆◆◆◆◆
Vertically centered, aligned, grounded: ◆

Under what circumstances or with what issues or subjects do you find your answers to be less accurate?

Asking same questions too many times, redundancy: ◆
Among skeptics, surrounded by people with negative thoughts,
in crowds: ◆◆◆◆◆
Blocking energies: ◆
Dowsing for others: ◆
Ego oriented, thinking with head, intellect, trying too hard:
◆◆◆◆◆
Emotionally involved, judgemental, personally involved,
personal predisposition, upset, emotionally charged issues:
◆◆◆◆◆◆◆◆◆◆◆◆◆◆
Family members: ◆◆◆
Future predictions, future issues: ◆◆◆◆
Getting irritated from answers: ◆
Geopathic zones, noxious energy: ◆◆
Health or personal nature questions for myself: ◆◆◆
Impatient: ◆◆
In a group: ◆

Lacking clear mindedness: ◆◆
Lack of real need, for myself: ◆◆
Locating missing objects: ◆◆◆◆◆◆◆◆◆
Locating missing objects for myself: ◆◆◆
Locating missing people, family members:◆◆◆◆
Lottery, gambling, speculation: ◆◆◆◆◆
Map dowsing: ◆◆
Mentally & psychically not "turned on:" ◆
Need to go through specific circumstances, growth opportunities for myself or for others: ◆
Non-serious questioning: ◆
Past lives: ◆
Political issues: ◆
Stress, anxious, time pressure, anxiety, tension, worry, being rushed: ◆◆◆◆◆◆◆◆◆
Questioning for others: ◆
Timing, time of day, time frame: ◆◆◆◆
Tired, tired, fatigued, ill: ◆◆◆◆◆◆◆◆
Unfamiliar objects, abstract: ◆
Violation of privacy or karma of others: ◆

To what do you attribute these difficulties?
Asking dumb questions on personal issues, for myself, lack of need: ◆◆
Astrological aspects: ◆
Can not clear mind, lack of focus, hurrying, not centered, emotionally upset, blockage of energy, not neutral, mind wandering: ◆◆◆◆◆◆◆◆◆◆◆◆◆◆◆◆◆
Change of perception or attitudes: ◆◆
Dowsing for too long at one sitting, not knowing when to stop: ◆◆
Emotional involvement, lack objectivity, personal pre-disposition, personal attachment, conscious control of outcome, ego involvement, too close to the individual: ◆◆◆◆◆◆◆◆◆◆◆◆◆◆◆◆
Environmental influences, earth changes: ◆◆◆◆
Fear of truth: ◆
Fear of giving wrong answers or bad news to others: ◆

Feeling out of "Sync", natural off cycles, bio-rhythms, not feeling well: ◆◆◆◆◆◆
Getting in over my head, beyond my abilities: ◆
Lack of confidence, self doubt: ◆◆◆◆◆
Lack of being open, not allowing it to flow: ◆
Lack of humility: ◆
Less interest, lack of need: ◆◆◆
Less familiarity with subject, not able to visualize subect: ◆
Need for more practice:◆◆◆
Need for more experience, information: ◆◆◆◆
Not able to connect with source due to distraction: ◆◆◆◆
Not asking the right questions: ◆◆◆◆
Not specfic questions, not accurate enough in questions, vagueness: ◆◆◆◆◆◆◆◆◆◆◆◆
Not phrasing question correctly: ◆◆◆◆◆◆◆
Not using proper protocol: ◆
Not really listening: ◆
Panic situations: ◆◆
Personal bias: ◆◆
Pressured into performing, pessure for results: ◆◆
Resistance, lack of belief with subject: ◆◆
Subconscious blocking energies that must be researched and cleared: ◆◆
Too open an attitude for my immediate environment: ◆◆◆
True answers not available: ◆
Using tool as crutch: ◆
Weather changes: ◆

What other problems, difficulties, obstacles, or challenges have you had in learning how to use and master the pendulum?
Alignment; spinal, psychic, planetary: ◆
Confusion : ◆◆
Deciding which hand was most appropriate to use (repressed left hander): ◆◆
Information coming in too fast: for pendulum response: ◆◆
Lack of concentration in presence of others or groups, picking up other's negative thoughts in close proximity:◆◆◆◆◆◆◆◆◆◆◆◆◆◆◆

Lack of consistency, unsure response: ◆◆◆◆
Lack of confidence: ◆◆◆
Lack of being able to achieve and maintain concentration: ◆◆◆
Lack of sincerity, not really wanting or needing the request: ◆◆◆
Learning detachment: ◆
Learning how to phrase questions accurately: ◆◆
Not all answers are ready to be given: ◆
Not having the wisdom, knowlege to use the pendulum for more things, solutions: ◆
Overcoming desired results, predetermination, clear mind of influencing thoughts: ◆◆◆◆◆◆◆◆◆
Pendulum heavier, respond better: ◆
Physically tired, fatigued, impatient: ◆◆◆
Polarity reversal of directions: ◆
Not being able to respond to intuitive answers when contrary to mental mind: ◆◆◆
Spirit effecting results, disincarnates, entities: ◆◆◆◆◆
Time of day: ◆◆

What solutions have you found to these problems, obstacles, difficulties or challenges?
Allowing enough time for energy to clear between questions: ◆
Ask another time or in another way: ◆◆◆◆◆
Asking the right questions, correctly, more accurately, rephrase the questions, asking from different angles: ◆◆◆◆◆◆◆◆◆◆◆◆◆◆◆◆
Asking the Source, connect with spirit, getting okay from higher self, faith, talking to God, prayer, inner alignment, guides: ◆◆◆◆◆◆◆◆◆◆◆◆◆
Avoid dowsing when emotionally upset, less emotional pressure: ◆◆◆◆◆
Avoid personal bias: ◆◆◆
Avoid self enrichment, keeping the ego out: ◆◆◆◆
Balance of right and left brain: ◆
Being with successful dowsers, more experienced dowsers: ◆◆◆◆◆

Believe in yourself, keeping confidence high, avoid self-doubt, trust myself: ◆◆◆◆◆◆◆◆◆◆
Check if the true polarity for yes/no: ◆
Checking and double checking answers: ◆◆◆
Clear mind, clearing self or area of negative energy, energetic toxicity: ◆◆◆◆◆
Clearing blocking energies, influences: ◆
Communication with others with more information, knowlege, experience, help, trust, dowsing group, practice with other dowsers: ◆◆◆◆◆◆◆◆◆◆◆◆◆
Conscious focused thought: ◆◆◆◆
Developing the feel for "the pull" in one direction or another, learn what if "feels" like to have a true answer: ◆◆◆
Dowsing only for beneficial and necessary information, others highest and greatest good: ◆◆◆◆◆◆
Dowsing in area free from interferences (geopathic, noxious energies): ◆
Dowsing when alone: ◆◆◆◆◆◆
Good procedure, form, good foundation: ◆◆◆◆◆◆
Heart connection: ◆◆
Journal my successes & proofs: ◆◆◆◆
Improve internal one focus, **clear intention**, keeping question the uppermost in my mind, concentration: ◆◆◆◆◆◆◆ ◆◆◆◆◆◆◆
Keeping myself open to all information, circumstances, guides information: ◆◆◆◆◆◆◆
Keeping a sense of humor: ◆
Learn from your mistakes: ◆◆◆◆
Learning to be very careful and specific in asking questions, making sure that the questions are completely understood: ◆◆◆◆◆◆◆◆◆◆
Learn how to get into the Alpha, Theta, & Delta brainwave frequencies: ◆◆
Learning to trust first with insignificant matters: ◆
Learning ways to increase concentration, avoid distraction: ◆◆◆◆◆◆◆
Learning detachment to outcomes: ◆◆
Meditation prior to dowsing: ◆◆◆◆◆◆

Practice, practice, pratice: ◆◆◆◆◆◆◆◆◆◆◆◆◆◆◆◆◆◆◆
Preparation: ◆◆◆
Polarity reversal of direction check: ◆◆
Qualifying questions: ◆◆
Remember May I, Can I, Should I and Is it appropriate at this time?, permission: ◆◆◆◆◆◆◆
Reading more literature on the subject: ◆◆◆◆
Shielding, prayer of protection: ◆◆◆◆◆
Studying books, learning, training: ◆◆◆◆◆◆
Taking deep breath, relax, calm: ◆◆◆◆◆◆
Teaching my ego to accept the intuitive answers as the best solution: ◆◆◆
Teaching others: ◆◆
Trust, trust 100%: ◆◆◆◆◆◆◆
Washing hands in cold water before using charts or percentages:◆

The Questionnaire Gems

The reason we chose to do a fill-in-the-blank type questionnaire is for the gems, the truths about form that came forth. We would like to close this chapter by offering you these gems of wisdom and form.

• Everything must come through the heart with confidence.
•When you dowse, you don't have to worry any more.
   David Darrow   N.Y.
• To challenge a failure leads to success.
   Anne Giardina   N.Y.
• I do a very methodical approach: I start by aligning myself thru spoken words, inner alignment to higher self. I ask permission to dowse = can I, may I, should I etc. I ask if I have any blocks to dowsing with higher self for 100% accuracy. If so, I ask that they be cleared until I know that I have a clear channel. Even after that, I check, double check, triple check all my answers with the source for percent (%) of accuracy.
   Pamela Colvin   ME
• Preparation: meditation...prayer...quiet time...drink ample water first in the morning...no food before...shielding with a holy ray of white light... clearing the pendulum, charts and

holy ray of white light... clearing the pendulum, charts & pictures with a magnet of clearing thought forms- asking the right questions. Write your questions on a 3X5 card using the same type specific, consistent questions. Washing hands in cold water before starting to use charts or percentages.

Start the pendulum with a neutral back & forth swing over the "O" then a round circle to the right for Yes and a round circle to the left for No. With this type of chart I can *feel a wall of resistance when the answer are changing* .

Thomas Mayer   AK

• I often pre-start the pendulum with a CC rotation and wait for a positive response or a directional swing. By starting at the edge of the map and watching for a swing that lines up with the target, I can "follow" the swing out into the map until the swing becomes a rotation. When following water flows and fractures, cross fractures and tributaries, can be indicated by quick changes in direction and continue the swing if you are going in the correct direction with the main flow. Stephen Bosbach   TX

We are most grateful to all of the American Society of Dowsers Chapters that responded to our questionnaire. The information provided, I'm sure, will be of great value.

- Armadillo Chapter
- Austin TX Chapter
- Blackhawk Chapter
- Blue Ridge Chapter
- Central New York Chapter
- Chittenden County Chapter
- Concord Erie PA Chapter
- Danville VT Chapter
- Dona Ana Dowsers of Los Cruces
- Dowsing Society of Kansas City
- Fairbanks, AK Chapter
- Finger Lakes Chapter
- Gold Country Dowsers
- Granite State Chapter
- Las Vegas Desert Dowsers
- Lone Star Chapter
- Manchester NH Chapter
- Michigan Chapter
- Northern Maine Chapter
- Puget Sound, WA Chapter
- Tennessee Valley Dowsers

I would also like to thank those individuals who put forth a great effort in helping others by contributing through their experience and expertise.

Conclusion

Throughout this book, I have shared with you many techniques to allow you easy access to the Intuition. With patience and practice, I believe you can successfully tap into your inherent dowsing skills. Your success will be dependent on your pendulum language, your beliefs, (whether expansive or limited) your technique, and *jeopardy influences* (whether external or internal).

Dowsing is like many other activities; *you learn more from your mistakes than you do your successes.* Each one of those mistakes must be understood as a positive step forward in the refinement of your dowsing skill. It is important that you make an effort to understand *why* a particular mistake occurred. What were you thinking at the time? Had your mind strayed from its image of the search? Had you made any incorrect assumptions? Realize that even though you may have made a mistake, you did receive a response to something. Your goal is to determine what that "something" was and why it was an error. The problem is not one of whether you can accurately dowse or not; it is one of refinement and clarity of the questions you formulate and the image you hold as you go through the physical dowsing process. All dowsers deal with erroneous results at various points in their dowsing careers. However, the frequency of error reduces with time as the dowser gains experience and becomes a clearer channel. Having a level of 80% or greater accuracy is definitely an accomplishment. In other words, it is okay to be less than 100% accurate with the results of your dowsing work.

Proof is sought as a mark of progress, and a track record of successes AND failures illuminates one's expansion into dowsing's many domains. Keep a logbook with the results of your exercises and experiments. In this way, progress can be noted and the areas that need work will be revealed. This record can also help you to discover the area in which you are the most accurate and proficient, and reveal a great deal about your own beliefs and personal growth.

Utilizing the Intuition with the intention of helping another person is much easier than one might think. The main ingredient is one's intention. With the proper perspective, an open heart and a loving, caring intention to help others, (with their permission), you can tune into another person anywhere in the world. Keeping yourself focused from your heart and brow center with your intention always for the highest and greatest benefit of others gives you a protective barrier of love and light that most often will allow you free access to the Infinite.

Dowsing is both art and discipline, and as such, you will benefit yourself and others by being as clear a channel as possible. This is where the discipline comes in. Daily personal growth work to identify, clear, and neutralize negative patterns, replacing those negative patterns with positive nurturing patterns, can only impact your life in an uplifting way—assisting you in your day-to-day living and also in your skills to externalize your Intuition.

Becoming involved in your personal growth work requires pranayama, or control of breath. This is the one thing that will assist you the most in your development. Your level of consciousness is directly related to your breath and how you breathe. It is the attention to breathing that is important. Deep meaningful breath, which has to be balanced both ways, in and out, is a necessity. Have you ever experienced some days when, so to speak, you were sitting there all day holding your breath? You forgot to breathe in/out, didn't you? When you get to the end of one of those days, you're usually exhausted from lack of oxygen and prana. Some of us hardly breathe at all. We breathe in, or we get caught in the world of fear or attraction and our breath almost stops totally. We have to remember every day, to take a little bit of time to breathe consciously. This is called self-remembering, and it is part of becoming more conscious of yourself, of the planet, and everything else. Stop and just take one breath and look and see what you haven't seen before in the space in which you are standing. Your reality in this world is strictly your impressions, and breathing consciously will open your eyes and your mind. Learning to breathe is a responsibility—a mandate, and is essential, if you are to work at these higher levels of consciousness.

We all have the ability to heal ourselves. The major difference between one person and another is limited or expansive belief systems. Some people hold more expansive belief systems, and because of this, they have higher levels of potential energy—they are able to transform the ever-present subtle energies surrounding them into healing energy for themselves or others. This transforming power is directly related to our breath— by breathing consciously we can enhance this energy system within our bodies.

Concentrating on our breathing—consciously raising our energy levels and our personal awareness—are the initial steps toward healing ourselves or others. (This is "remembering" our innate healing abilities.) This is the first step in changing consciousness. Changing consciousness is like tossing a pebble into still water; the pebble drops, and circles emanate out from the center. This is the effect that raising our consciousness will have on the world around us.

The responsibility to change consciousness lies with each individual. How do we change consciousness? Begin by eliminating negative beliefs. Take responsibility for your own life. Release old patterns, vicious circles, imprints, and debilitating conditioning. Replace those old patterns with new, positive, and nurturing patterns. Raise your energy level by conscious breathing, meditation, affirmations, and visualizations.

Consciousness is awareness, an internal perception. The state of consciousness from which we view the world and interact with it is crucial. The state of our consciousness determines the world as we know it, both what we perceive the world to be, and what we project to contribute to that world view.

Reshad Feild says that we are transformers of subtle energy. But realizing that there are many stages of development, we want to know what kind of transformers we are. How clear are our channels? How well have we polished the mirrors of our hearts? If we as dowsers wish to be of service, at what level do we understand service? How close is our service to reflecting Divine Love? Those great beings who manifest at that level communicate health and life by their presence alone. We are most fortunate, for we have been made aware, through learning to dowse, of the divine spark within everyone. We have been made aware of our potential to move beyond what we had accepted as the limitations of our world in a progressive expansion of consciousness which is really only limited by the limits we put upon it. *"The only limitation my mind has is belief in its limitation,"* said Dr. Abdui Aziz.

Dowsing is about seeing at a distance—beyond the five physical senses. As we climb a mountain, we get a wider view. And so it is with the expansion of our consciousness beyond that of our own personal, limited egos. Becoming a better dowser means learning better how to live in harmony with the earth and all she supports. To do this is to develop planetary consciousness. It means expansion through learning the divine intention and then helping to manifest it as transformers of subtle energy. Discovering the divine intention and helping it to manifest that is what service and helping are really about.

By helping people to question, perhaps by dowsing, and to explore their context, we assist them in developing a perspective concerning their relationship to a larger whole. We may be able to help them see what is behind some of their problems. This awareness of cause will help them to release these problems, a process which will in itself be healing.

Dowsing is an expression and merging of the ego self with that great sea of the divine heart—the drop in the ocean *and* the whole ocean emerging as the drop. It establishes our awareness that our actions spring from that sense that we are both part of the whole and the whole. As we become aware of this amazing heritage of the human being, it becomes our responsibility to manifest that awareness to the degree of our understanding of it in all that we do.

Albert Einstein wrote,

A human being is a part of the whole, called by us the "Universe," a part limited in time and space. He experiences himself, his thoughts and feelings as something separated from the rest— a kind of optical delusion of his consciousness. This delusion is a kind of prison for us, restricting us to our personal desires and to affection for a few persons nearest to us. Our task must be to free ourselves from this prison by widening our circle of compassion to embrace all living creatures and the whole of nature in its beauty [1]

The practicing neophyte dowser now fine-tunes the newly acquired skills in responding to calls and demands, whether in the framework of a job or a personal need. The realization comes that all things are connected; the mineral, plant, animal, and soul kingdoms form a vast network of relationships which are intertwined, each affecting the other. This creates a feeling of self worth and a responsibility to those being served.

With these higher dimensions of thought, many dowsers become what might be called apprentices, dedicated to the development, continued study, and the art of dowsing. Visions on all levels; the physical, emotional, mental and spiritual become more perceptive and the inner life more powerful and peaceful. Ideas; gifts from the Intuition, enlighten the mind with ways of helping and healing. The individual no longer feels isolated or separate, but instead, a part of the Greater Whole. There is a sense of freedom, expansion, and communication with all other Souls and the Universe. The dowser, we might say, becomes a co-creator in the plan, beginning to build new thought-forms of goodwill, love and understanding, generating these energies throughout the planetary network, thereby transforming and becoming transformed in the process.

We can see that throughout the different stages of dowsing we can greatly affect the planet and all that live therein. Although the idea of interconnection is certainly not new and has been a part of the spiritual teachings of all the great traditions, it is a concept that seems periodically to need to be rediscovered. We have had many warnings in the past thirty years of the ecological folly of our applications of pesticides and disposal of sewage and industrial chemicals, polluting the water and poisoning the land and causing the infusion of heavy metals, pesticides, and other harmful chemicals into the food chain. Now is the time when we simply have to wake up to our responsibility. It is easy to avoid the issues by saying that it is a superhuman job to clean up the waste, the pollution, and the appalling things that we've done to our cities, mountains, rivers, streams, and even our oceans themselves. I'm sure, however, that given sufficient knowledge and an open heart, we can find ways to help.

Geomancy is the process of bringing man's activities into harmony and resonance with the earth and with the cosmos. How much do we need to know about this before we act? The web of relationship is probably much more intricate than we can understand, and so we ask permission of the Source and ask that anything we do may be harmonious and within the balance of nature. There are many practical things that can be done, but the most profound changes come from helping to change consciousness. Though we can do something, this does not mean that it is appropriate to do so or to the highest good to do it. Remember the four questions asked first.

Always ask:

May I?— Am I permitted?

Can I? — Am I able? Do I have the skill to do this?

Should I? — Is this the time? Am I the one to do it?

And as a final check, "Is this the truth?"

If, for example, we cause to be moved a water vein that reads "harmful to health," without permission, we may well affect our neighbor's water supply to trees needing water. We might even have an affect on the lightning pattern as it appears that lightning strikes particularly on the crossing point of water veins. Our actions affect the greater whole of existence—and it is our mandate as responsible dowsers to be aware and compassionate. Our dowsing can have far-reaching implications. As we realize our part in the greater whole, new worlds of awareness open to us. We look beyond the five physical senses and see new potentials within ourselves for our personal benefit, for the benefit of others, and for the benefit of our planet.

Can you really be a good dowser without possessing some level of planetary consciousness? I do not think so. How can you do distant or map dowsing unless you have some kind of planetary consciousness? Dowsing encompasses a wholistic philosophy— a philosophy of one-ness. That is also what planetary consciousness is about. It is about the integrating of the ego into the heart of universal consciousness. It is the perceiving— through an awareness of the whole—of the right relationship of the parts to the whole, and assisting in creating that harmony. Striving toward planetary consciousness means working toward expansion of your own consciousness, releasing it from the prison of separation, and realizing its limitlessness.

As you start to develop a planetary-consciousness, you will become a better dowser, and you will become a custodian of your own planet Earth, which at this time in history, is very much in need of your help and awareness.

Dowsing is an intuitive art—a means to externalize your own Intuition. The Intuition is a bridge between the conscious self and the Infinite Intelligence, Wisdom, the life force of all creation. By learning to use your Intuition, you can have a positive and beneficial impact on yourself, on others, and on the planet on which we depend for our survival. The rules of the road are easy. Where thought goes, energy flows. The more we link up with the intuitive and infinite part of our being, the more we will identify with it, the more we allow its energy to flow through us and fill our mind with light, our hearts with love, and our hands with wisdom and power, the richer, simpler, and better our lives will become.

I have attempted to impart some tools and some practical wisdom and truths to assist you in your day-to-day living. If used properly, the Intuition and its tools, will teach you how to improve the quality of your life tenfold.

By knowing your intuitive mind, you can come to know and understand yourself better in all realms of existence that span the physical, mental, emotional, and spiritual realities. By knowing your intuitive mind, you can relate more fully to the source of creation. Practice the techniques in this book and let the tools, and your Intuition, teach you what is for your highest and greatest good in all that you do, so that you may be of benefit to humanity and life in all its forms. You are embarking on a wonderful and exciting journey of self-discovery. Enjoy!

Get Intuit,! If In Doubt, Check It Out.

Come visit our webb site: http://www.get-intuit.com
To Write to the Author
We cannot guarantee that every letter written to the author can be answered, but all will be forwarded. Both the author and the publisher appreciate hearing from readers, hoping for your enjoyment and personal benefit from this book. The author sometimes participates in seminars and workshops, and dates and places are announced in the Crystalline quarterly bulletins. To write to the author with your intuitive experiences, to ask a question, or to be put on the bulletin mailing list, write to:

Dale W. Olson
P.O. Box 2088
Eugene, OR 97402 U.S.A

[1] Michael Nagler, *America Without Violence*, p.11.

Bibliography

Archdale, F.A., *Elementary Radiesthesia, and the Use of the Pendulum.* The British Society of Dowsers, 1950.

Bachler, Kathe, *Erfahrungen einer Rutengangerin,* Veritas Verlag, Linz, Harrachstrasse 5, W. Gmy., 1981. (Translated by Marianne Gerhart: *Discoveries of a Dowser*).

Bachler, Kathe, *Discoveries of a Dowser,* (English translation), p.204.)

Beasse, Pierre, *A New and Rational Treatise of Dowsing according to the methods of Physical Radiethesia.* Mokelumne Hill, Ca.:Health Research, 1975.

Bentov, Itzhak, *Stalking The Wild Pendulum.* N.Y.:E.P. Dutton, 1977.

Besant, A., & Leadbeater, C.W., *Thought-Forms.* Il.: Theosophical Publishing House, 1971.

Bhattacharyya, Benoytosh, *The Science of Cosmic Ray Therapy or Teletherapy.* Calcutta, India:Firma KLM Private LTD, 1976.

Bird, C.,& Tompkins, P., *The Secret Life Of Plants.* N.Y.:Avon Books, 1973.

Bird, Christopher, "Dowsing in the United States of America: History, Past Achievements and Current Research." *The American Dowser*, vol 13, no.3, August, 1973, pp. 105-6.

Bird, Christopher, "Finding It by Dowsing," *Psychic,* Vol.VI, no.4, September/October, 1975. pp. 8-13.

Bird, Christopher, *The Divining Hand*. E.P. Dutton, N.Y., 1979, p.270.

Blackburn, Gabriele, *The Science and Art of the Pendulum: A Complete Course in Radiethesia.* Idylwild Books, 1983.

Brennan, Barbara Ann, Hands Of Light:*A Guide to Healing Through the Human Energy Field.* Bantam Books, 1987.

Cameron, Verne L., *Map Dowsing.* Elsinore, CaEl Cariso Publications, 1971.

Chapman, E.C., *The 12 Tissue Salts.* Jove Publications, 1979.

Cox, Bill, **The Techniques of Pendulum Dowsing.** Forces, 1977.

Davis Ph.D., Albert Roy, *The Anatomy of Biomagnetism.* Fl.:Davis Research.

Detzler, Robert E., *Your Mind Net,* Redmond, Wa., 1988.

Finch, W.J., *The Pendulum & Possession.* AZ.:Esoteric Publications, 1975.

Graves, Tom, *Dowsing and Archaeology*. Turnstone Press, 1980.

Greene, Linda L., *Learning the Secret Language,* Samaitan Foundation, Edmond, Ok, 1990.

Judith, Anodea, **Wheels of Life.** MN:Llewellyn Publications, 1987.

Kopp, Dr. Joseph, **Transactions of the Swiss Society of Science**, Ebikon, Switzerland, 1970. pp.253-255.

Kopp, Dr. Joseph, "Children's Illneses Due to Soil Influences", **Prophylaxe,** Central Pamphlet For Social Hygiene, Ebikon, Switzerland, Sept. 1970, Vol.9.

Leadbeater, C.W., **The Chakras.** London: Theosophical Publishing House, 1974.

Mermet, Abbe', **Principles and Practice of Radiesthesia.** London:Watkins Publishers, 1935.

Nielsen, Greg & Polansky, Joseph, **Pendulum Power**. Excalibur Books, 1982.

Nadel, Laurie, **Six Sense,** The Whole Brain Book of Intuition, Prentice Hall, New York, 1990

Oregonian, "Are Electrical Lines Powering Cancer?", Kurt Sternlof, August 6, 1987.

Purce, Jill, **The Mystic Spiral,** Thames & Hudson, 1974.

Ramacharaka, Yogi, **Science of Breath**. Yogi Publication Society, 1904.

Raphaell, Katrina, **Crystal Enlightenment.** Aurora Press, 1986.

Raphaell, Katrina, **Crystal Healing.** Aurora Press, 1987.

Ross, T. Edward and Wright, Richard D., **The Divining Mind,** Destiny Books, Vermont, 1990.

The American Dowser, Vermont: American Society of Dowsers, 1960-1975

The American Dowser, Spring 1988 Volume 28, No.2, Herbert Douglas, p24.

The American Dowser, Volume 28, No.4, 1988, The Resonance Factor, T. Edward Ross,II, pg. 9

The American Dowser, 1991, Volume 31, Dowse A House, Richard Perrott, No.1, p.16

The American Dowser, Winter 1991, Vol.31 No.1, Understanding and Dealing With Dowsing Failures, Steven G. Herbert.

Vogel, Marcel, *Psychic Research Newsletter.* Ca.:Psychic Research, 1974-1990.

Wayland, Bruce & Shirley, *Steps to Dowsing Power.* Life Force Press, Inc., 1976.

KNOWING Your Intuitive Mind

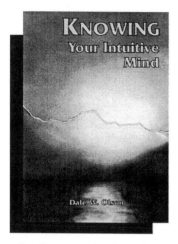

by Dale W. Olson

In this landmark book, Dale W. Olson takes the reader on an encouraging and inspirational journey using ancient and modern Intuitive technologies to access your whole brains potential. With straightforward and measurable techniques you learn to use various tools, exercises and skills to externalize the Intuition. Most of all, this process gives the readers the confidence to be free from a "trial-and-error", or guessing approach to life.

Quality paperback 196 pages **ISBN #1-879-246-00-7**   **$14.95**

Book Reviews

Knowing Your Intuitive Mind is one of those rare inspirational gems. This an excellently written book, full of new approaches and wonderful reminders about developing ourselves to enjoy a more intuitive whole life.   *-Michael Peter Langevin*   **Magical Blend**

A milestone work that answers, "What the Intuition is, how it functions, and through the use of examples, teaches us how to develop our communication between the various aspects of our mind." "The Intuition serves as a bridge. If used properly, the tools and the Intuition will teach you how to improve your quality of life tenfold." "Knowing Your Intuitive Mind" by Dale W. Olson is filled with love and compassion and surely illuminates the path to empowerment and enlightenment.
                    -Richard Fuller   **Metaphysical Reviews**

I found **Knowing Your Intuitive Mind** interesting, informative and very practical. In a very clear manner it gives a good background to the intuition and how it works. Author Dale Olson presents a well-balanced and levelheaded approach with well explained drawings and pictures. I heartily recommend this powerful book. It will take the reader on a journey that allows them to know and understand themselves better and help them gain confidence in their creative ability to change. *-Martha K. Dane, Ph.D*   **Better World**